ECONOMICS
MADE SIMPLE

D0910853

ECONOMICS MADE SIMPLE

How money, trade and markets
really work

MADSEN PIRIE

Hh

HARRIMAN HOUSE LTD

3A Penns Road
Petersfield
Hampshire
GU32 2EW
GREAT BRITAIN

Tel: +44 (0)1730 233870
Fax: +44 (0)1730 233880
Email: enquiries@harriman-house.com
Website: www.harriman-house.com

First published in Great Britain in 2012

Copyright © Harriman House Ltd

The right of Madsen Pirie to be identified as the Author has been asserted in
accordance with the Copyright, Designs and Patents Act 1988.

ISBN: 978–0857–1–91427

British Library Cataloguing in Publication Data
A CIP catalogue record for this book can be obtained from the British Library.

Set in Minion and Gotham Narrow.

Printed and bound in the UK by CPI Group (UK) Ltd, Croydon, CR0 4YY.

for Tyler Beck Goodspeed

CONTENTS

ABOUT THE AUTHOR

Dr Madsen Pirie is President of the Adam Smith Institute (**www.adamsmith.org**) and Senior Visiting Fellow in Land Economy at the University of Cambridge. He was awarded the National Free Enterprise Award in 2010 (jointly with Dr Eamonn Butler). He frequently appears as a commentator on television and radio, and has published articles in most major national newspapers and magazines. Madsen often addresses university and school audiences on economic and policy issues, and occasionally participates in panel discussions and speaks at international conferences. He is a graduate of the Universities of Edinburgh, St Andrews and Cambridge.

Other books by Madsen Pirie

Think Tank (2012)
101 Great Philosophers: Makers of Modern Thought (2009)
Freedom 101 (2008)
How to Win Every Argument: The Use and Abuse of Logic (2007)
The Sherlock Holmes IQ Book (with Eamonn Butler) (1996)
Boost Your I.Q. (with Eamonn Butler) (1991)

For young adults

The Emerald Warriors (2011)
Tree Boy (2011)
The Waters of Andros (2007)
Children of the Night (2007)
Dark Visitor (2007)

www.madsen-pirie.com

ACKNOWLEDGEMENTS

6

I am most grateful for the help I received in the preparation of this book. Anthony Haynes made invaluable suggestions that made the book much more user-friendly, while Sam Bowman and Paul Woods were kind enough to read through early drafts and make constructive suggestions to improve it. Other much appreciated help came from Tom Clougherty, Sally Thompson and Jean-Paul Floru, and from my colleague Eamonn Butler.

Needless to say, any errors, imperfections and inadequacies in this book lie entirely at my own door.

1 INTRODUCTION

EVERYDAY ECONOMICS

E CONOMICS IS VERY MUCH in the news in today's world. In ways that would have been inconceivable a half century ago, we are made aware that much in our daily lives depends upon economic events. Our standard of living, our ability to afford the things we value, our future prospects, and eventually our pensions are all influenced by economic activity. Some of this takes place close to home at a personal level, but some events happen in distant places, set in motion by people we will never meet.

Economics is all around our everyday lives, yet much of it seems opaque and mystifying to ordinary people. Commentators appear on our screens or in the pages of our newspapers, and make pronouncements about what they believe has been happening and will happen, and much of what they say seems arbitrary and baffling.

There has probably never been greater interest in economics, given global financial crises and domestic downturns. People are aware that what happens in financial news will affect them, and many of them wish to know how and why. Some see their spending power going down; others face the possible loss of their job. They want to know the reasons such things are happening.

Professional economists are rarely helpful. Some affect a jargon which makes their subject esoteric and inaccessible, such that meaningful discussions can take place only with their colleagues. Many academic economists have retreated from the real world into mathematical models which purport to show relationships between past data, but tell us little about the present and nothing about the future.

Yet the essentials of economics are not difficult to understand or explain. The subject is not a science like physics or astronomy, and can never be so because its subjects are human beings, independently motivated and quite capable of changing their minds and the way they behave, unlike the atoms and stars of the physical sciences.

Economics is about human behaviour. It is about the ways we have developed for dealing with each other in complex relationships. It is about how people whose time and resources are limited choose to allocate those resources, and how they interact with others to do this as effectively as they can manage.

No individual or group sat down and 'invented' economics by setting out the principles that govern our exchanges. Economics was certainly devised by humans, but not consciously or deliberately. It developed naturally out of the ways people developed for dealing with each other and with their resources. It is a natural outgrowth of human personality and social co-operation.

The complex relationships and institutions of modern economics all have their origins in the ways we interact with each other, and in how we choose to live our lives.

The aim of the following pages is to introduce the subject of economics in ways that non-economists can readily understand. Without jargon or complex equations, the aim is to show how easy and intuitive the subject can be once its fundamentals are understood. Welcome to the world of economics.

Madsen Pirie
Cambridge, 2011

TRADING THINGS,
CREATING WEALTH

"**S**plash!"

A smile cracked across the old man's walnut-stained face as the sleek bird broke the surface. He could see the silvery fish, its tail glittering as it writhed in the cormorant's throat. Good. That made six today.

Black Silk was his favourite bird. As it fluttered onto the end of his boat, the old man stroked its head affectionately and took the fish from its beak. He untied the ring from the bird's throat and rewarded it with a couple of smaller fish which the bird eagerly snapped up. His weather-beaten eyes took in the sun, now low in the sky. Six was enough. With a contented sigh he bound the remaining fish to his pole with the others and headed for the shore.

The market was already beginning to break up as dusk neared, but he knew that the stall he wanted would still be in business. Sure enough, the stallholder greeted him with a quick smile and a bow, a flash of interest lighting up his eyes as they flicked to the six fish on the pole over the old man's shoulder.

After courtesies were exchanged it was time for business. The old man held out the day's catch for inspection. The stallholder's eyes narrowed as he inspected each fish, looking at the bright eyes and clear, silvery skin. Finally he pointed to a bag of rice at the back of his stall. A patient smile flitted across the old man's face as he shook his head. He pointed to a larger bag of rice next to the small one. The stallholder hesitated a moment, gave the fish another quick glance, then smiled himself and nodded. The deal was done, the exchange made. The old man strolled off contentedly. It had been a good day, and Black Silk had earned him a two-week supply of rice.

The stallholder rubbed his hands as he walked off. He knew just the person who would reward him handsomely for such excellent fresh fish. He was right, too, for the restaurateur spent only moments examining and prodding the fish before producing a wad of currency and peeling off some notes. Once again there were bows and mutual smiles as the exchange was made. The restaurateur chuckled inwardly at the thought of how those fish would look later that night, dressed and cooked, on the plates of his diners, how delighted his customers would be, and how many extra meals he'd be able to sell.

SCENES SIMILAR TO THESE are played out every day in hundreds of millions of ways. Some are small-scale, such as those involving fish and rice, but others can run into billions of dollars as whole companies change hands. Human beings trade. It is part of what it means to be human that we seek to add value to our lives. The 18th century father of economics, Adam Smith (1723–1790), described what he called "the uniform, constant, and uninterrupted effort of every man to better his condition," and it applies equally to women. We seek to improve our lot, to enrich our lives, and this is why we trade.

There is a common misconception that in any exchange there must be a winner and a loser. We speak of someone 'getting the better of a deal', as though the other person has come off worse, but this is mistaken. A trade takes place when we give up something we value less in exchange for something we value more.

Each of the parties to a deal would rather have what the other person has than what they already have themselves.

We value things differently. We have different personalities and preferences, different tastes and priorities. It is part of the diversity of the human species that we do not all want identical things to the same extent. Even the things that we do all seek, such as food, allow for an enormous variety of preferences; some of us prefer meat, some fish, and some fruit.

It is because we value things differently that exchanges take place. The fisherman in the above example wanted the bag of rice more than he wanted the fish, whereas the stallholder wanted the fish more than the rice. Each therefore gained from the exchange; that is why they did it. The same is true of the other characters in the story. The restaurateur wanted the fish more than the money in his pocket, whereas the stallholder preferred the money to the fish. The exchange gave each of them something they valued more highly than what they already had. The diners later that night would pay for their suppers because they valued the meal more than the money it would cost them, while the restaurateur would happily hand over the food because he valued the money more.

Creating wealth

Far from there being winners and losers in an exchange, both parties gain. Trade is thus a win–win situation of benefit to both sides. Something else is true as well: an exchange makes both parties richer. After the trade each party has something more valuable than they had before. It is because they set a higher value on it that they traded in order to acquire it. They now own greater value, which means they are richer.

Riches are often measured in terms of money, but they need not be. Someone who pays money to attend a concert or visit an art gallery is adding value to their lives in non-monetary ways. They find the cultural experience of more value to them than the money was, so that parting with the money has gained them something they thought worth more.

Since people trade in order to gain something of higher value to them, the more that they engage in trade, the greater will be their gain in value. People become wealthier by trading with one another because trade creates wealth. In the above illustration, the fisherman had his fish and the stallholder his rice. Both became richer by the act of exchange. It was the exchange itself that gave both of them extra value. Neither of them gained additional value by taking it from the other; they created it between them by their action.

Some people falsely suppose that wealth is fixed, and that people can only become richer by making others poorer. They think of wealth as being like a pie, where someone taking a larger slice leaves less behind for others to enjoy. This is not the case. Additional wealth is created by the act of trade, and trade generally makes all of its participants wealthier.

The reason why people in advanced economies are richer than their forebears is not because they went out and took wealth away from other people. It is because they created wealth by trading, wealth which was not there before. Poor countries are not poor because someone has robbed them; they are poor because they have not created sufficient wealth.

Some people are concerned to study and to understand what causes poverty, but even the question is a misconception. There are no causes of poverty – it is simply the absence of wealth. Poverty is the default condition; it is what happens when you do nothing. Most of humanity for most of its history has been poor, living precariously at subsistence level. The unusual condition is wealth, and that came about through exchange and trade.

People in prehistoric times probably traded flint tools for furs, starting the process of wealth creation by adding value to their lives. Agriculture and animal husbandry brought with them a much greater ability to store value, and provided many more opportunities for exchange. Trade caravans crossed deserts and merchant ships crossed oceans as cargoes were exchanged and wealth created. Cornish tin miners would reportedly set piles of tin on the beaches for passing Roman galleys. The Romans would land and leave bundles of goods in a proposed exchange. If there were not enough to satisfy them, the miners would take some of the tin away until eventually the exchange satisfied both parties. The trade took place with no language in common, and no cultural interaction beyond the trade itself. Yet both parties gained something they valued more, and co-operated in making each other richer.

Specialisation

The diversity of humankind gives us different talents and abilities. Some of these come to us through the accident of birth, and some are acquired by learning, and by putting in the hours and years of practice required to hone us into skilled practitioners. It means that we all do different things with different degrees of skill.

The old man in our story had developed and perfected the ability to fish with his cormorants, and could count on it to bring him the rewards of his skill and labour. The stallholder knew how to run a market stall, what goods would be demanded and in what quantities. He knew how to bargain and set prices for his goods that would bring him economic returns. Whoever grew the rice knew the ins and outs of agriculture, what seeds to use, when to plant them and how far apart, how to irrigate the growing shoots, and when to harvest them. The restaurateur knew how to provide cooked meals for his customers, what they would want to eat, and how it should be prepared and presented to satisfy them.

All of these are different skills, and all of them involve the use of different types of ability. None of us can be good at everything; we have neither the natural abilities nor the time it would take to develop and polish them. It is exchange that allows us to specialise. Specialisation enables us to live far better than we ever could if we relied only on our own abilities. We would almost certainly catch fewer fish than the old man with his cormorants – if, indeed, we caught any at all. If we planted and tended our own rice, we would certainly produce less of it than a skilled farmer could manage. And so it goes on throughout the activities that sustain us and add value to our lives. In almost every case we have access to more goods and better goods than if we tried to produce them all ourselves. The specialisation, which exchange makes possible, brings the services of experts to work for our benefit.

Specialisation also brings efficiency. The skilled fisherman can catch more fish in a day than an amateur, just as the skilled cobbler can make more and better shoes, and the skilled baker can bake more and better bread. Through exchange we are able to draw upon products made by those with greater skills than our own, and thereby to enjoy a higher living standard than we could have managed by relying solely on our own skills.

The experts will usually find ways of operating with greater efficiency. They will develop the shortcuts and acquire the fluency to enable them to produce more in a day than an amateur could hope to. If it takes them less time, they will often be able to charge prices that are highly competitive compared to what it might cost us in time and effort to do it ourselves.

Specialisation gives us access to goods produced more efficiently than we could make them ourselves, increasing our wealth even more than simple exchange already does. Furthermore, specialisation can take place not only between different occupations such as fishermen, stallholders and restaurateurs. It can also take place within each occupation, enabling further increases in efficiency.

The shoemaker might work with a son or daughter, with one of them making the parts of the upper shoe, and the other concentrating on the soles of the shoes. In this way each can develop and polish the skill to make part of the final product. Another son or daughter might become expert at stitching the finished parts together, with each performing the part of the production process they do best. They will almost certainly produce more shoes between them than they would have done if each of them had made whole shoes.

Adam Smith pointed to a pin factory in which it took 18 separate operations to make a pin. "One man draws the wire, one straights it, a third cuts it, a fourth points it, a fifth grinds it at the top for receiving the head", and so on. A person on their own needing to perform each of these operations might make at most 20 pins in a day, and perhaps not even one. By specialisation a group of workers could make many more between them. Smith spoke of a factory where ten men each performed a task, with some doing perhaps two or three operations, and they managed to produce 48,000 pins in a day, averaging 4,800 pins per employee. This is vastly more than any of them could have managed individually.

Of course, the customers of those pins, given that kind of specialised efficiency, have access to them at far lower prices than could have been offered by any individual pin-maker. And the manufacturer has far more stock to sell, and far more potential customers to sell to. Wealth has been created by specialisation, as well as by exchange.

Mass production

The American inventor Eli Whitney (1765–1825) played two important roles in wealth creation. First, he invented the cotton gin, a mechanical device to separate the cotton fibres from the seeds, a time-consuming process when performed by hand. It enabled each worker to produce fifty pounds of cleaned cotton in a day. This made cotton cheap and plentiful, and gave people of modest means access to good quality and affordable clothing.

Whitney's second contribution is one for which he is less famous, but which has had more lasting significance. He looked at the muskets made for the US army. Each one could be crafted by an expert gunsmith, who could, by specialisation, produce more muskets and better muskets than any amateur could hope to make. But Whitney went one stage further, and looked for opportunities for further specialisation. Whitney's idea, which has reverberated through industrial societies ever since, was that the muskets could have interchangeable parts. One worker could shape the barrels, another one the stocks, another the flintlocks, another the triggers, and so on. A musket could be made by fitting together any barrel with any stock, with any flintlock and any trigger. Whitney won a huge contract to supply muskets to the US Army, and the age of mass production was born.

Henry Ford, creator of the Model T car which brought motoring within the means of the average American, is widely credited as the instigator of mass production. In fact it was the moving production line he pioneered. Eli Whitney introduced mass production over a century before him. Mass production enables workers to concentrate their skills on making single components, thereby bringing the greatest efficiency. In the pin factory written of by Adam Smith, each stage a pin went through in its manufacture was undertaken by a differently skilled worker in turn; in Eli Whitney's gun factory, every stage of manufacture could be undertaken separately and simultaneously. The result has been products that add value to people's lives at low cost, contributing hugely to the wealth creation achieved by modern industrial societies.

There has been a further element to the generation of wealth achieved by exchange and specialisation. It is mechanisation, the application of external power sources to the production process. It began with water, with mill wheels alongside rivers driving the machines that made textiles in Britain's early industrial revolution. Then came coal, which powered the machines of Victorian England, and then electricity which was applied throughout production in the early decades of the 20th century.

The application of power was made possible by specialisation. Once the production process had been divided into separate and distinct operations, it was possible for external power, be it water, coal or electricity, to lend strength and speed to the elbow of the working man or woman.

A continuous story of trade and exchange can be told. It started with the exchange of furs and flints as people traded up for what they preferred. It continued with specialisation as people concentrated their energies on what they did best, and traded their products to secure their other needs. It carried on through specialisation of the separate parts of the productive process, with people honing their skills and efficiencies on one component of a product's make-up. It reached its modern form with the use of interchangeable components and the application of external power.

People trade. They do so to gain value, and they specialise so they will produce more goods to trade with. They introduce efficiencies in order to produce more goods for their input of time and resources, and they do this so they will have more to trade with, and more opportunity to add value to their own lives.

Some modern commentators have called the whole process of wealth-creation into question, suggesting that enough is enough, and that perhaps people should be satisfied with simpler lives instead of constantly trying to improve them. People do seek to improve their condition, as Adam Smith observed, but wealth is not an end they pursue for its own sake; it is a means by which people improve their lives. It is the creation of wealth by exchange and specialisation that has removed millions of people from wretched lives devoted to simple survival. The wealth generated has lifted people from starvation. It has conquered many diseases and is conquering more. It has provided the means for widespread education. It has enabled societies to care for those unable to fend for themselves. It has funded the spread of knowledge and science. It has enabled people to afford better transport, habitation and sanitation. People in poorer countries do not want to lead simpler lives; they want to improve their own lives and have access to the choices and the chances available to those in richer nations.

Wealth brings opportunities in its wake and it helps humanity to solve its problems. It enables people not only to lead better lives, but also to reshape their own lives with its opportunities. It is created by the simple acts of exchange and specialisation, but the possibilities it unfolds are limitless.

WHAT THINGS ARE
WORTH, AND WHEN

"If I had a million pounds," declared Jane, "I'd spend about a thousand pounds a week and enjoy living really well." Adam snorted, doing a quick calculation in his head. "You'd be broke after 20 years," he retorted, "and then you'd be destitute."

"No," replied Jane. "I'd buy bonds paying 5 per cent annually, which would bring me £50,000 a year. Then I'd have to spend about £1,000 a week to avoid getting any richer. After 20 years of spending £1,000 a week, I'd still have the million pounds left, and I'd still have an income of £50,000 a year."

ONE OF THE MISTAKES into which language leads us is the idea that things have some kind of value existing independently of our desire for them. They do indeed have value, but it is not a property of the object like its length, breadth or depth. Unlike those properties it is not something that can be measured in ways we all agree upon. This is because the value of something does not reside in the object but in the mind of the person who contemplates it. And because we have different minds, we value things differently.

Something can be highly valued by one person, and yet be thought worthless by another. A prime steak, suitably aged and perfectly cooked, might be highly valued by one gourmet food critic, and yet regarded with distaste by another who happened to be a vegetarian. That is because the value lies not in the steak but in the mind of the beholder. These differences in how different people value things are what makes trade possible, with its gain in value by both sides and the consequent creation of wealth.

When people mistakenly suppose that things have an independent value which does not depend on how highly people rate them, they can easily be led into other mistakes. They ask how the object came to have that value, and suppose that the value must have been put into it or added to it at some stage of its manufacture. Karl Marx (1818–83) supposed that an object's value ultimately derived from the labour it took to make it. If raw materials were involved in its manufacture, their value could be reduced to the labour it took to extract or collect them. If machines were required to make it, their value derived in turn from the labour it took to make them. Everything's value was, he thought, a measure of the labour involved in its production.

Marx went further, building a whole critique on this false step. If the price charged for an object is greater than the labour cost it took to produce it, he said, this profit represents 'surplus value', and is created by cheating the workers out of the full value of what they have produced. Marx called this "exploitation" by the manufacturer or merchant, and condemned the entire system that allowed it.

Other analysts have taken a slightly more complex view by saying that an object's value derives from other factors as well as the labour it represents. Some have suggested that most production involves some use of land, which they say cannot be reduced to labour. Others have pointed to capital investment, the money put in to pay the costs of producing things, as a necessary requirement. All of these examine value from the point of view of the provision of something, examining what it takes to make it.

In fact value derives from the demand for an object, rather than from the factors involved in its supply. If no one wants the finished object, it does not matter how much went into its production; it still has no value. Someone can allocate a great deal of land, labour and capital to produce an object, but if no one wants it, then it is literally worthless. In practice this limits what will be produced. If the value people will set on an object is below that of the inputs it takes to produce it, it will not generally be made.

The truth is that articles are regarded differently by different people, regardless of what it takes to produce them. People compare them with other articles they have or desire, and rate them higher or lower according to their different standards and judgements.

It is also true that people value things differently under different circumstances and at different times. Obviously a person crossing a desert might value water more highly than someone at home who can obtain it simply by turning on a tap. It might, indeed, be the same person who values it less at home than on a desert trip. Many of us tend to value something more highly when it is newly acquired, and to value it somewhat less when the novelty has worn off. We might value heavy jackets and shoes more highly at the onset of winter, but rate short sleeves and sandals more highly as spring turns towards summer.

Taking account of time

Time is an important element of how we value things because people generally value immediate gratification more highly than pleasure which has to be postponed. If we offer a child a choice between one chocolate now and one chocolate tomorrow, we would generally expect the choice to be made for immediate enjoyment. There is no reason why a child would want to prolong unnecessarily its period of doing without chocolate. It is when we offer the alternatives of one chocolate now or two chocolates tomorrow that the choice becomes interesting.

Other things being equal, an immediate pleasure is more highly valued by us than a distant one. The immediate one is more certain, because no one can know what might happen in the intervening period to thwart our future enjoyment of the distant one. It can also be enjoyed without waiting, as can the memory of it afterwards.

Since the distant one is less valuable, some extra value must be added to it to make it preferable; we have to be paid in extra value for giving up our immediate gratification. Hence arises the choice between one chocolate now or two of them tomorrow. People respond to this in different ways, with some going for immediate satisfaction, and others surrendering instant pleasure in return for greater gain in the future. The decision made depends to some extent on the character and circumstances of the person making it.

Some commentators point to the influences of a person's educational and social milieu in making such choices, with those more highly qualified or from wealthier backgrounds apparently more ready to defer present enjoyment for future gain. Social analysts call this a person's *time horizon*, suggesting that those from poorer circumstances have a short one, being more likely to avail themselves of immediately accessible benefits, while those higher up the social or educational scale have longer ones, and are more likely to perceive value in saving up for greater returns later on.

It is because the distant return needs to have something added to it to bring its value beyond that of the immediate return that the notion of *interest* arises. The £100 spent now will give pleasure immediately as I spend it on things I value more highly than the money. If I have to spend time without the gain in value I could have enjoyed, I will expect to be compensated by receiving a greater value.

If I lend the £100 to someone for a year at 5 per cent interest, I am saying that I prefer the £5 extra value to compensate me for the year spent without my £100. The person who borrows it is someone who values the £100 now more than the £105 in a year's time. It could be someone who expects to receive money in the intervening period, or someone who hopes to use my £100 to make more than £105 within a year.

Although some religions have condemned the practice of lending money at interest, its basis is that of a straightforward payment to compensate the lender for postponing the pleasures their money could bring in the intervening period. As with other exchanges, it is one that benefits both parties; the one wants the money now and will pay extra to obtain it, whereas the other is happy to part with it in return for the interest payment offered.

When friends lend each other money they usually do so without charging interest. This is because the value of doing a friend a favour, or of helping them out, is thought adequate payment for doing without the money in the intervening period until it is repaid. With strangers, however, or people we will never meet, the interest payment constitutes the added value that motivates us to engage in the transaction.

When we put money in a bank account, we are lending it to the bank. The interest the bank pays is our compensation for temporarily foregoing the immediate pleasures we could buy with the money. Our motive is that we would rather have the future added value, plus the security of keeping our money in what we hope and believe are safe hands. The bank's motive is equally straightforward. It pays us to entrust our funds into its hands because it believes it can use the money to earn it more than the interest which it will pay us.

Banks do not keep our deposits locked up in their vaults. If they did, we would have to pay them for looking after it for us, for they would have no other motive to do so. They would certainly have no reason to pay us interest on monies that were simply locked away in their vaults; why should they? It is because banks make use of our money when we deposit it with them that they are able to pay us interest out of the profits they make on it.

Some banks make money on the cash people deposit with them by lending it out to others at a higher rate than the interest they themselves offer to depositors. Banks can be a source of finance to businesses, especially to ones starting up that need cash to tide them over until they become profitable.

Risks and rates

The interest demanded by lenders does more than compensate them for postponing their own enjoyment for the period of the loan. It also has to cover the risk that they might not be repaid.

Anyone who lends money takes a risk. The borrower might be unable to repay the loan when required to, quite apart from the interest on it that was promised. In general, the greater the risk of default, the higher will be the interest charged. The lender has to estimate what proportion of borrowers might not repay, and charge interest rates sufficiently high that those who do repay will cover the losses on those who default, and will also pay the required interest.

Different classes of borrowers will be charged different interest rates, reflecting the different risks involved. Starting up a small business is quite a risky affair, given the numbers that do not succeed. The interest rates they are charged reflect this. On the other hand, public bodies such as Treasuries or local government authorities are reckoned to be relatively low-risk borrowers since they are ultimately backed by taxpayers, and rarely go broke. This is why they will usually pay lower interest rates than small businesses will have to pay.

One way for small businesses to lower the interest rates they pay is to offer collateral on the loans they take out. They nominate something of value, such as the title deeds on a property, which will be surrendered if they default on the loan. Given this backing, the risk of loss to the lender is substantially reduced, so he or she will be able to charge significantly lower interest rates. In most cases the collateral is simply pledged, so that in the event of a default on the loan, the borrower will have a legal right to seize the property which was offered as security against it. Given this right, a much lower interest rate can be charged, since the borrower is carrying most of the risk of default.

In some cases, notably those involving pawnbrokers, the collateral property is physically handed over to the lender. A pawnbroker will take property, for example jewellery or expensive watches, and lend the customer somewhat less than its resale value. If the loan is repaid in time, plus an agreed interest sum, the customer reclaims the property. If not, it is forfeit, and the pawnbroker recovers his or her money by selling it.

When their resources are expended on immediate pleasure, people gain the value of the experience. When they defer that for future reward, their resources are increased, and with them the potential for more of the valued experiences. The postponement of our immediate gratification thus plays an important role in wealth-creation.

Postponing gratification

The person who lends money at interest is foregoing the present consumption in which they could engage in order to gain more resources to spend later. They are investing in order to accumulate wealth. They can do this because other people want to borrow, and are prepared to pay for the privilege. Investment is about putting resources to work, using them to generate more resources instead of enjoying them immediately.

The early hunter-gatherer who spent time fashioning flint spearheads when he could have been out collecting berries or pursuing animals was in effect investing time. Instead of deriving immediate gains, he yielded these in order to achieve the larger gains that his flint-tipped spears would make possible in the future. The farmer who uses time that could have been spent on idle pleasures in ploughing and sowing is similarly investing for the rewards to be gained when the harvest is in.

People accumulate wealth not only by trade and exchange and the specialisation which accompanies this; they also do so by committing part of their present resources towards the acquisition of greater resources in the future. All investment involves a kind of self-discipline and denial, a preparedness to make do with less now in order to acquire more later. Character and culture play a role in this, in that some societies and social groups seek to impart these qualities to their young, teaching them through proverbs and stories the wisdom of self-denial in pursuit of greater gains in the future.

It is not greed or selfishness which makes people seek to multiply their resources through investment. On the contrary, it represents that desire of every person to better their condition, to add value to their lives, and depends on their ability to do without now in exchange for anticipated future benefit.

Investment works because resources can be used to generate more resources. It can be used, for example, to fund specialisation by paying for machines that can increase the output of each worker. That increased output means that more goods can be produced, and at a lower cost per item. This in turn opens up the possibilities of greater sales and profits, and that, in turn, makes it possible for the investment to be repaid with interest, and still leave the borrower substantially better off.

Costs of business

Most new businesses require investment, often by the person starting them up. There are premises to be bought or rented. There is equipment to be used and supplies to be obtained. Take the simple case of someone who wishes to set up business as a window cleaner. They might be able to run the business from their home or garage if local by-laws permit such use; otherwise they might need to rent a shed. They will need equipment in the form of buckets, mops and ladders. They will need some kind of transport to reach their customers' addresses, meaning that a car, van, or at least a bicycle will be needed. There might be supplies to be bought, such as detergents. And of course they will need customers, which means advertising, perhaps by leaflets dropped through letterboxes or posted on local noticeboards. There might be training required in the skills and safety drills associated with the task.

Unless the would-be window cleaner has sufficient savings to cover these costs, money will have to be borrowed, and there will be interest to pay on the loans. There are various government-backed schemes to help such initiatives, but it might come down to persuading a lender to put up money, maybe requiring some kind of collateral to act as security, or even a guarantor who pledges to repay the loan in the event of a default.

The lenders defer their enjoyment of their money in order to earn more of it, and the window cleaner invests time and effort in the hope of building up a business that will bring in future gains, foregoing present pleasures in order to do so. The business will probably take time to build up, perhaps operating at first with returns that do not cover its costs. The hope is that sufficient customers can be signed up to provide the window cleaner with a steady cash stream that enables the initial costs and loans to be repaid, leaving a viable business in place. If it succeeds, wealth will have been created in the process. The proprietor will have used resources to generate more resources, and the investment will have succeeded.

Although matters are more complicated for larger businesses, the elements are very similar. Investment is required to achieve higher future returns, and the money has to be found somehow, often by borrowing. Time has to be factored in, as with most economic calculations, and people will have to be paid interest for doing without the use of their resources for the time it takes for the anticipated returns to arrive. For larger businesses, in addition to the costs of premises, equipment, transport, supplies and marketing, there will be the labour costs of paying wages to staff. This is often one of the greatest costs, and has to be met even though no returns are yet being received.

Alternative uses

There is another factor involved in investment. The investor certainly needs to be compensated for the enjoyment which the money might have brought otherwise, but he or she also has to consider the alternative uses to which the money might have been put during the same period. When we use money on one thing, we are deciding not to use it on something else instead. Every use of it takes the place of what might have been done instead. This is usually true of time as well as money. Time we spend doing one thing cannot also be spent doing another, except in the rare cases where several things can be done simultaneously. Time spent at the races might otherwise have been passed at the cinema or a restaurant. We cannot do all three at the same time.

In the case of money, we have to consider what might have been done with it otherwise. Just as we cannot spend the same money on a bicycle and a coat, so we cannot put the same money into different investments. If we buy bonds from a government Treasury, we cannot use the same money to loan to small businesses. This is called the *opportunity cost*, referring to the opportunities which are excluded when one use is chosen. Some of those alternative uses might have involved immediate enjoyment on new clothes or a pleasure cruise, but others might have involved putting it to use to generate even more money.

The use we choose for money denies us those alternative uses and we have to take account of them, including the greater money that some of them might have made.

If I invest £4,000 on a solar panel for my roof, I look forward to savings on my annual electricity bills. But I might have invested that money instead in bonds bringing an annual interest of 5 per cent, or £200 a year. That was an opportunity cost, so in addition to the £4,000, I am also giving up £200 a year in interest I could have made. My electricity bill savings will need to be at least £200 a year before I even start to make any real savings.

I might then factor in the expected lifetime of the panel before it needs to be replaced. How long will it survive the rain, hail and frost? Maybe 20 years would be optimistic. This means I am using up my £4,000 at the rate of £200 a year, so my bill reduction needs to be at least £400 a year (including the interest I could have earned) before I even start to make any savings.

The rule to remember in all of this is that every activity takes place at the expense of what could have been done otherwise. The time spent on one activity cannot also be spent on another. Money used to buy one article cannot also buy another. And investment in one area uses up the resources that could otherwise have been invested elsewhere. Economics is about choices, and in addition to the decisions we make in economic activity, we also have to take into account the ones we could have made.

PRICES, SELLING
AND BUYING

AMONGST THE EARLY examples of human writing are those which survive from the Babylonian Empire of the ruler Hammurabi, approximately 4,000 years ago. Hammurabi was a lawgiver as well as a conquering emperor, and the *Code of Hammurabi* ranks alongside the law codes of Justinian and Napoleon as one of history's greatest. In amongst the 3,600 lines of cuneiform script carved on a pillar found at Susa, and referred to among the innumerable clay tablets that survive from his period, are the maximum prices allowed by the law for a whole range of commodities, and the appropriate wages to be paid for various occupations. A few examples serve to convey its flavour:

> "If a man hire cattle, wagon and driver, he shall give 180 qa of corn per diem."

> "If a man has hired a wagon by itself, he shall give 40 qa of corn per diem."

> "If a man hire a field-labourer, he shall give him eight gur of corn per annum."

> "If a man hire a herdsman, he shall give him six gur of corn per annum."

> "If an ass has been hired for threshing, ten qa of corn is its hire."

> "If a man hire a 60-ton boat, he shall give a sixth part of a shekel of silver per diem for her hire."

Most of the prices and wages were involved with agriculture, given its importance to the Babylonian economy, but the code set wages and prices in other areas. The pay of potters and tailors was set at five grains of silver, whereas for carpenters and rope-makers it was four grains. The code even covered healthcare and veterinary services:

> "If a physician set a broken bone for a man or cure his diseased bowels, the patient shall pay five shekels of silver to the physician. If he be a freeman, he shall give three shekels of silver. If it be a man's slave, the owner of the slave shall give two shekels of silver to the physician."

> "If a veterinary physician operate on an ox or an ass for a severe wound and save its life, the owner shall give to the physician 30 grains of silver."

The detail is impressive, even specifying what payments are to be made on behalf of the different classes in society. Hammurabi is not widely regarded as an arbitrary and capricious ruler; on the contrary, he is seen by many as an enlightened administrator who sought to improve the lot of his people. It is a reasonable assumption that the prices and wages set out in his code are ones that would have been regarded in his day as appropriate reward for the items or services specified. They corresponded, perhaps, to what might have been regarded as fair.

A 'fair' price

Hammurabi might well have been one of the first to establish and stabilise fair and just prices for everyday transactions, but he was by no means alone. History echoes with the voices that have called out the definitive worth of things and the prices that should be paid. The theologian Thomas Aquinas thought there should be a just price for things, generally settled, and the idea remained popular in the mediaeval world and into modern times. Even in the second half of the 20th century, governments in both Britain and the United States passed legislation to set wages and prices at what they considered to be reasonable levels.

None of these ideas of fair or just prices seem to allow for variation or change, depending on the quality of the item or the circumstances prevailing at the time. In Hammurabi's code, for instance, a field labourer receives eight *gur* of corn per annum, regardless of how diligent or skilled he is at his task. The herdsman is paid six *gur* of corn per year however attentive he is to his animals, or no matter how careless he is of their welfare. In a real economy, as opposed to instructions carved out on a pillar or written into a statute book, one would expect that those who delivered greater value might be able to command higher pay.

The 60-ton boat seems to cost a sixth part of a shekel for a day's hire, no matter what its condition might be. A new boat or a faster boat, or perhaps even more, a safer boat, might be worth more than an old sluggish one that ships water. Despite their differences, the law rates them the same. Again, in a real economy one might expect quality to command a higher price.

The law can stipulate, as it did, that a physician should receive five silver shekels for treating a freeborn citizen, three for a freed slave, and two for a current slave, but no one should be surprised if they found that physicians preferred to treat freeborn citizens if they could, spent rather less time on freemen, and devoted only cursory attention to slaves.

There is also a problem that prices fixed by law cannot change over time as circumstances change unless the law itself is changed.

The fixed price for a bushel of corn might seem reasonable during years of good harvests, but if a few lean years come along with lower yields, farmers might find it hard to make a living unless the price is allowed to change.

The whole concept of a fixed price, a fair price, or a just price supposes that the price should reflect some arbitrarily established value of the item. Different individuals value things differently, however, and will be prepared to surrender different amounts in exchange for them. Since there is no fixed value, there can be no fixed price. If there were such a thing, who would be able to ascertain what it was? Some people value an item more highly than others do, and will give up more in order to obtain it.

Taking circumstances into account

Price is not a reflection of any intrinsic value something might have, nor is it the sum of what it cost to produce it. It is instead what the owner will demand in order to part with it. This will usually be greater than the costs of production, otherwise the item would not have been produced at all, but there are cases when things are sold at prices below production cost, such as when stock is sold off cheaply to clear space for more profitable items.

In real economies prices are not fixed by decree. They vary according to circumstances and location, and sometimes even according to who is buying. A cup of coffee at a café round the corner will probably cost less than a cup of coffee at the Ritz Hotel, and a cup of coffee at the top of Mount Snowdon might cost even more than that.

In many countries of the world there are no set prices at all, since they are subject to bargaining. An initial asking price is met by an initial offer, and only after bargaining takes place will a price acceptable to both be struck. The price depends to some extent on how good at bargaining both parties happen to be, but it might also depend on how good a day it has been for the seller, and what resources the buyer can spare. It is also common in popular holiday destinations for affluent tourists to be asked to pay higher prices than those sought from less well-off local residents.

Given that prices vary so much over time, and according to circumstances, location, and the status of the customer, the question arises as to why lawgivers from Hammurabi onwards have tried to fix them. The answer is probably that lawmakers are earnestly trying to protect their citizens from the hardship caused when prices rise during periods of shortage, especially shortages of food. If food prices rise in a period of famine, people struggle to make ends meet. It seems at first glance to be unjust that some should benefit from high prices at a time when others are suffering. The call to limit the profits made by corn merchants in a famine will always find ready ears among poorer people, and among legislators who try to act in the best interests of their subjects.

Lawgivers who fix prices by statute might indeed be inspired by honourable motives, but motives do not fill empty stomachs, and we have to ask what actually happens when prices are set by law, rather than by buyers and sellers. Paul Samuelson in the sixth and seventh editions of his book *Economics* gives this cautionary tale:

> "There were in Flanders two kingdoms. In Zig, good king Jean commandeered the food brought to the city in time of famine, paying the peasants a just (but generous) fee and rationing supplies in fair shares for all. As the famine persisted, the dying citizens blessed the dying king.

> "In nearby Zog, at a time of plenty each of a dozen merchants stealthily built (and stocked with cheap grain) a warehouse of food. When famine came, they sold the food at double the usual price, stripping people even of their watches and jewels. Some (but by no means all) of the jewels they then gave to the less-hard-hit peasants to coax out still more food; and as the news spread, peasants came with food from as far away as Zig. The longer the famine, the higher the price the Zogites paid for food, until finally the market rationed them to a minimal diet. By the time the famine ended, the whole city was in debt to the merchants, but alive; and each merchant was resentful that competition from his colleagues had kept him from increasing his fortune twentyfold, rather than only fourfold."

In Zig, where fair prices were paid for food, the supply dried up and the people starved, along with their fair-minded ruler. Farmers were not prepared to supply any more at the fixed (low) prices. In Zog, where no fair prices were legislated, there were large price rises, big enough to attract farmers, even distant ones, to supply more food. The people grumbled, but they lived.

The story is a fable, but it illustrates an important point. It is that prices have an existence and a function beyond the well-meaning intentions of the legislator. They convey information and they provide incentives to action.

In the story the rising prices conveyed the information that food was in short supply. They told the merchants that they could afford to pay more for their own supplies, and they told the peasant farmers that Zog was the place to send their food. The higher prices coaxed more food out of them, and brought it in even from distant places.

People acted to improve their own lives, but the result was to bring enough food into Zog to keep the inhabitants alive, while those in Zig starved, even though they thought it was fairer. They met this fate because their well-meaning ruler had prevented prices from sending out the information about shortages, or providing the motivation for people to redress it.

The rules prevailing in Zig might be thought fairer, but economics is not about fairness but about the allocation of resources. In Zog the prices sent out signals that there was not enough food to meet people's needs, and their levels motivated outsiders to do something about it. They brought in more food and the famine eventually ended. In Zig the prices were prevented by law from doing this.

Who does set prices?

If prices are not to be set by lawmakers, the question arises as to who does set them. The answer is a strange one; it is that no one consciously undertakes the duty of setting them. They emerge instead through countless transactions and decisions made by individuals. A seller declares how much money he or she would prefer to have than the articles on sale, which might be, for example, a range of coats. Buyers who value the coats more than that amount will complete the exchange, and those who value the coats less than that will stay away. The sum at which the transaction takes place is the price, but it is transient. In another town or on another day it might be different. Prices are not fixed; they change with time and location.

Even prices which appear to be fixed, such as those which manufacturers print on their products, are subject to variation. The price might be written on a book or a chocolate bar, but not everyone pays it. Some will buy their books online from discounters, and some will buy their chocolate bars from supermarkets plugging price reductions to attract customers.

Instead of trying to reflect the value of things, what prices do reflect is their relative availability. When many people all want something in short supply, they in effect bid against one another. If there are ten items available and 100 people want them, the seller will be able to set a price such that the items will go to the ten buyers prepared to pay the highest price.

The opposite happens when there are plenty of items available but not many people want them. In such cases the sellers are effectively competing with one another to set prices low enough to attract customers. They want to sell their stock, but since potential customers have plenty of sellers to choose between, those sellers must lower their prices to persuade customers to head their way instead of shopping elsewhere.

Even though prices convey information about shortages and surpluses, and even though the signals they send motivate people to act, these do not happen simultaneously. As with so many things in economics, time enters into the equation. In some cases higher prices for goods can motivate people to put more of them on the market fairly rapidly. This can happen where goods are stored in warehouses, for example, and it only requires organised effort to bring more of them out of storage and transport them to where they can be put on sale.

Committing resources

In most cases additional goods have to be produced first. Most manufacturers do not like to store large quantities of goods, for this involves tying up resources into producing goods to sit idle in stores, when they would prefer to sell those goods at a profit and then produce more of them. To produce more goods usually involves committing more resources. Sometimes this can be achieved by taking on additional staff or by working factory production lines for longer hours. Very often it will involve the expansion of production by investing in new plant and machinery, and even new premises.

All of these take time. In most businesses new staff are not hired overnight; there is a recruitment process and interviews to be done. Even a factory reorganisation to augment output will usually require time to plan and implement. When it comes to investment in new plant and premises, the time lag is even longer. Observed price rises can signal that there is scope for increased production to take advantage of them, but the time that it takes to respond to those signals can be weeks, months, or even years, depending on the type of business and the degree of preparation needed. In cases of food shortages, for example, it can often take a year, or at least a season, before the crops in short supply can be augmented by new planting and harvesting. In some cases the shortfall can be filled by imports from new foreign sources, if the laws allow this or can be changed to do so. Otherwise it means waiting for a new season and a new harvest.

Since it takes time to bring extra production and supply on line, some shortages signalled through higher prices may persist for some time before actions succeed in redressing them. And the action of producing new supplies in response to shortages is by no means automatic or risk-free. The potential producer has to ask if the shortage is likely to persist long enough to keep prices high until the new production can go on sale. He or she will usually be committing investment in plant, equipment and personnel, and does so on the basis of prices that may not last.

Some producers will undoubtedly expand production in response to price increases, only to find by the time they have committed resources to it and actually started to ship the new goods, that prices have not held up, and the anticipated returns are no longer to be had. As in other cases where producers have to anticipate future demand and future prices, the rewards tend to go to those who are right more often, or who are simply luckier.

Anticipating behaviour and events

Producers have to take account of the likely behaviour of other producers, as well as of consumers. If the price rise caused by a shortage leads many other suppliers to increase production, prices may come down faster than expected, and anticipated gains fail to materialise. A producer might respond to a shortage by trying to be among the first to bring new supplies to market, hoping to cash in before rivals bring their own increased production on line. Or he or she might decide not to invest in new production at all, calculating that too many others will be trying to do the same.

Agriculture is a case where the lead time it takes to increase supply can lead to massive mismatches between supply and demand. A shortage of one crop, such as peas, for example, might result from harvest failure caused by poor weather or a virulent parasite. The resultant price rise might signal to farmers that there is good money to be made from peas, and many of them might increase their acreage devoted to peas in consequence. Improved weather and better pest control might bring about a bumper harvest of peas as a result. While this will benefit consumers by redressing the shortage and bringing prices down, it will not be as beneficial to those farmers who committed extra resources and time that they might have committed to alternative crops. The bumper harvest which brings lower prices for consumers also brings lower profits for the farmers.

Cases could occur in which shortages cannot be redressed because production cannot be increased. A new industrial process, for example, might use rare minerals or chemicals and send prices for them heading upwards. These are not manufactured items whose production can be stepped up, but raw materials that occur in nature and have to be extracted. Normally a shortage and its attendant price rise would send surveyors and mining engineers looking for extra supplies, even ones previously untapped because at the old prices they were not worth extracting. But there might simply be no other sources of supply available, and no way in which the price rise can be countered by extra supplies of them coming onto the market.

There is still a likely effect caused by price rises, even when no extra supply is forthcoming. Most items we use have things that can be substituted for them, even if the replacements are less efficient or lack the quality made possible by the original. A shortage which induces a price rise sends its signals that more of the substitutes should be used, even though they might be less efficient. They were perhaps not worthwhile at the old price of the primary commodity, but they become so when its price increases.

Increases in the costs of production also send researchers scurrying to their laboratories in the attempt to develop cheaper substitutes. The rapid development of fibre optic cables owed much to increases in the price of copper as demand for it steadily outstripped supply. The high copper prices sped up fibre optic research and led to cables which could be used to do the same job at a fraction of the cost.

How prices provide information

Prices are an essential way in which individual decisions by buyers and sellers act to convey information. That information, transmitted through markets, enables resources to be allocated more efficiently. It enables people to act to redress shortages, and encourages them to do so. It tells people that they should use less of commodities that are in short supply, and should use cheaper substitutes if these are available, and try to develop some if they are not.

There is at least one further thing that price does: it tells people how to use resources to generate maximum value. Just as any economic activity takes place instead of, and at the expense of, the other economic activities that could have been done in its place, so any use of a resource takes place at the expense of what it could have been used for instead. The steel that goes into a car cannot also go into a ship, a kettle or a fence. It has to be used for something, and price plays a large role in deciding what that shall be.

Any exchange is of something which is valued less in return for something valued more. Whatever the steel adds more value to will generally command a higher price for it there. If it adds greater value to a car, for example, than to other things, this will usually mean that the car maker can command more of it by being prepared to pay a higher price for it than can the makers of those other things. In general, resources will go to those prepared to pay more for them, and these will tend to be those who add more value to the finished product.

Thus prices play an important role in directing resources to uses in which they add the most value. But this only happens if they are allowed to send their signals. Where prices are set by legislators and rulers instead of by markets, the information will be lacking about where resources add greatest value. The prices set might be thought 'fair', but they will not act to redress shortages, or to allocate resources to where they add the most value and are used to the greatest efficiency. The process of wealth-creation is impeded whenever prices are set by law instead of by the real priorities which people express through their purchasing decisions.

PRODUCING AND DISTRIBUTING

T wo men paused to look over the fence at the huge construction site going on below the street. Below them was a hive of activity as construction workers swarmed over the site. In the centre of it all was a huge mechanical digger scooping up great piles of earth and mud and piling it in onto a conveyer belt to have it sent upwards and conveyed away in dump trucks.

One man eyed the mechanical digger sourly and remarked to his friend, "That mechanical digger has taken away the jobs of 12 men who could have done the work with spades."

"Indeed," replied his friend, "and each of those spades would have taken away the jobs of 100 men who could have done the work with teaspoons."

THE ELDERLY CHINESE man fishing with his cormorant is a producer. He does not make the fish, of course, but in catching them and bringing them to the market he introduces them into the economy. Similarly the farmer who grows rice is a producer; he or she creates a product that was not there before and trades it to those who value it. The restaurateur who buys food ingredients and turns them with skill and labour into meals is also a producer, adding value by inputs to produce something worth more than the various constituents it took to make it.

The diners who buy meals from the restaurant are consumers, and they are at the end of the economic process and the reason it takes place at all. If there were no consumers there would be no producers. The things that are produced are done so with consumers in mind; their purpose is to satisfy buyers and to persuade them to part with their cash because they would rather have the product than the sum of money it takes to acquire it.

Production achieves many things. It provides jobs, and wages that go with those jobs. It enables people to provide for their families. It provides the means whereby people can save to afford worthwhile things such as housing and education. It engenders an extraordinary range of products that enhance or simplify the lives of those who use them. But all of these achievements are contingent on the presence of consumers. It is the buyers at the end of the chain who provide point and purpose to the activity. Adam Smith put it succinctly: "The end of all production is consumption."

People do not produce for the sake of producing; they produce with consumers in mind. Coal mining or steel-making provide much-valued jobs to the communities in which those industries are located, but that is not their purpose. There would be little point to mining coal or producing steel if they were simply piled up in giant mounds and never used. If they were simply stored, there would be no revenue forthcoming to pay the wages of those who worked in those industries, or to pay for the machinery and equipment used in their extraction and manufacture.

It is because there are consumers who want to buy the coal and the steel, or the products made from, or made possible by, those ingredients, that their production takes place at all. The money paid by consumers who value those products passes down the production and supply chain, and ultimately pays the wages of those engaged in their manufacture. Indeed, the demand of consumers, or their anticipated demand, plays a large part in determining whether production will take place at all. It is the expectation of payments by consumers that justifies the investment in plant, equipment and personnel to commit to production in the first place.

Bringing new goods to market

The fisherman with his cormorant and the rice farmer both bring onto the market things that were not there before. This is what, on a larger scale, the deep-sea fishermen and large-scale farmers also do. The fish are there to be collected by the application of labour, skill and appropriate equipment, and the crops can be planted, nurtured and harvested from the soil. It is what coffee planters and fruit farmers do, and is similar in some ways to what miners also do. The miner extracts minerals from the earth as the fisherman catches from the sea and the farmer generates from the soil, and all of them bring their production to be sold on the market.

This is not the most common type of production, however. The bringing of completely new products taken from nature or the environment is only one type of production. Much of modern production involves taking simpler materials and using them to manufacture more complex ones which have more value.

A farmer might grow cotton and introduce it onto the market, but it serves as the raw material for a host of production processes which add value to it and create different products derived from it. The common feature of all of these manufacturing processes is that there are consumers willing to pay for the end products.

There are spinners who will turn raw cotton into thread that can be sold. There are weavers who will use that thread to make rolls of cotton fabric to be sold on. There are garment makers who will use those rolls of cotton to make clothes, and there are at intermediate stages various people who will add value by treating and dying the fabric. There are designers who use their artistic and creative skills to produce garments that people will be eager to buy.

The cotton farmer might produce the original product from nature, but there are many producers who start further down the production chain, each adding value that will be paid for by other producers who will add their own value in turn. The one thing that unites all of these producers is that they are producing goods whose ultimate target is the consumer. Their immediate consumers might be other producers who use their output as raw material for the next stage, but at the end of the road is the person who buys the ultimate product, the consumer whose satisfaction motivates the entire activity.

Adding value

A common feature of the production process is added value. Producers take objects as their inputs, and process them in ways that improve their value to consumers. The additional money that people are prepared to pay for the improved objects covers the cost of the original inputs, the cost of the process they undergo, and sufficient reward to the producers to make the whole exercise worthwhile from their point of view.

Production is a risky activity. Given the time it takes to bring goods to market once the decision has been made to produce, there is a great deal that can go wrong. The prevailing prices on which the decision was taken may not last, and could fall by the time the goods reach the market. They might no longer be high enough to bring in anticipated returns high enough to cover the costs which had to be committed. There could be changes in supply brought about by other producers entering the market in the intervening period. There might be changes in demand brought about by altered weather patterns or even natural disasters.

Even if prices do hold up until the new production reaches the market, they might not last, as other producers rush out their own production. The would-be producer has to take a gamble as to what market conditions will prevail at the time the new goods reach the market, and how long those conditions might last. The return on the activity has to be sufficient to cover the risks involved. Sometimes, even if the prices do hold up until the new supply reaches the market, the producer has to recover the costs of production quickly, calculating that profit margins will not last.

The high prices which tend to accompany shortages are never popular with consumers. They often regard such prices as 'unfair', thinking that producers are taking advantage of supply shortages to jack up prices and make excessive profits. They see the high prices without realising their role in bringing extra supplies onto the markets, thereby easing the shortages. They see the prices being charged without seeing the investment that has been committed or the resources allocated to increasing production.

The terms used to describe such prices carry with them the air of general disapproval. The term 'profiteering' is used to indicate the making of what are regarded as unjustified and excessive profits. The term 'windfall profits' suggests that they are unearned, and occur simply by chance. The activity of putting up prices in times of shortage is sometimes described as 'price gouging'. The language used to describe such activity is indicative of the sense of unfairness which it provokes. Prices serve to allocate scarce resources, though, not to impose moral values on them. They help to redress shortages, which they cannot do if they are arbitrarily fixed by legislators.

In addition to the elusive 'fair prices' talked of by legislators since Hammurabi of Babylon, there are also what some economists call 'equilibrium prices', but they are just as elusive. As the demand for goods interacts with the supply – the quantity available for purchase – some observers think that there is a price at which all of the supply on offer is taken up by all of those wanting to buy. This is the point, they say, where demand matches supply, and this price they call the 'equilibrium price'. A higher price will see some goods unsold, whereas a lower price will see empty shelves with unsatisfied customers still clamouring to buy. Only at the 'equilibrium price' will supply and demand match each other.

Rough and tumble of markets

This concept of an equilibrium price might look good in the pages of learned papers, but it does not tell us very much about what happens in the real world with its rough and tumble of constantly changing prices and preferences. In the real world supply never does meet demand, and there are no settled prices. Everything changes constantly as different people make different decisions to buy or not to buy, to raise or lower prices, to save, invest or spend. It is all in constant motion, adjusting from day to day and even moment to moment. The price never settles, nor does the supply of goods or the demand for them. At best there might be long-term trends which see prices move up or down over time, and items become relatively more scarce or more readily available.

The price of fish on the Eastern market of our example might alter according to how many fish the old man caught that day. It might depend on how much rice the farmer managed to grow that season, or on how many diners are in the mood to eat fish that night. These factors change all the time, and because many of them depend on the whims of human nature and its preferences, they are inherently unpredictable.

We should note that one of the characters in our story did not himself produce any of the goods which he traded. The fisherman produced the fish, aided by his cormorant. The distant farmer whose rice was exchanged for them grew the rice, and the restaurateur produced meals for the hungry diners. The stallholder, however, did not personally produce either the fish or the rice which he traded for each other. He was a middle-man, coming between the producer and consumer.

Middle-man, not bogey-man

The role of the middle-man has rarely been properly understood by the general public, and perhaps for that reason has rarely been popular. People see the middle-man (or woman) as someone who buys goods for less than he or she sells them for, without adding anything to them in the process. The goods seem to pass through their hands unchanged, with no visible extra value added to them. Not surprisingly, people think of this activity in a poor light, regarding middle-men as people who charge consumers more than they paid themselves for the goods.

Those involved in selling direct from factories or manufacturers often tell us that the cost of goods can fall if we 'cut out the middle-man'. If people were to buy directly from the factory, the claim is that the margins charged by middle-men could be eliminated. The wholesaler, who buys in bulk from the manufacturer or importer, and the retailer who buys in smaller units from the wholesaler, can both be bypassed, we are told, and prices reduced accordingly.

In fact middle-men (and women) perform a useful service which requires marketable skills. The middle-man makes sure the goods are available to the public in the varieties they want, at the quality they seek, and in locations that are convenient to them. They have to pay for premises and staff, and invest in stock. They have to make sure that they estimate correctly what the public will want to buy and when they will want to buy it.

The business is highly competitive, since most customers have the option of shopping elsewhere. Unsold stock represents wasted investment that could have been more profitably employed elsewhere. Skilled middle-men are very good at calculating how much return they must seek on each square foot of shopping space, and what mix of goods will increase both their returns and the satisfaction of their customers.

The invisible value they add to the goods that pass through their hands is *convenience*. The public would find it very difficult to shop if they had to buy everything from the manufacturer. The manufacturer would probably have to raise prices to cover the extra costs of dealing with the public directly. Middle-men have survived throughout history because, far from being parasites who add nothing to goods, they enable them to reach wider markets in ways that are convenient for consumers. They are the link that connects producers and consumers who might otherwise never even find each other, much less meet each other's needs.

Convenience

It is true that the spread of internet access has made it more possible for people to buy some goods direct, but even these are more usually from some more sophisticated middle-man than from the producer's warehouse. Companies such as Amazon act as middle-men between publishers and book buyers, and have been replacing some of the trade which formerly went to bookshops, another group of middle-men. They do this with a huge variety of other goods, too.

The convenience added by middle-men can be that of a local store or of doorstep delivery, and they enable consumers to browse, either through a real shop-window or through the virtual shop-window of an internet site.

However useful that convenience may be, it is unlikely to change the popular perceptions about middle-men that have endured for thousands of years. People can see the value added when seed is turned into rice, or when fish is turned into delicious cooked dinners, but the value added by convenience is invisible; people cannot see it. To them the goods look the same when they leave the middle-man as they did when they arrived. The dealer seems to be getting something for nothing, and the buying public often has a lingering resentment to that.

The mark-up of the middle-man looks to the general public suspiciously like a tax that puts up the price of goods without contributing to their production. In fact the middle-man usually adds a real and valuable service.

Customers would have to spend much time and effort in locating and arranging to purchase the goods they require were it not for the invisible value added by the middle-man. That added convenience is usually delivered efficiently, at low cost, and in a consumer-friendly way. The reason for this is that the middle-man lives in a competitive world. His customers can go elsewhere if his prices are too high, or his selection of goods on offer is inferior. The competition and the threat of it keeps his activity lean.

There is one type of middle-man who comes in for particular opprobrium from the general public. People might reconcile themselves to the convenience provided by retailers and dealers, and convince themselves that the mark-up they pay is a worthwhile exchange for the added value of convenience. But no such benevolence is directed towards speculators.

Speculators

If one were to list the professions most detested and despised by the public at large, it is quite likely that, up there with politicians and tabloid journalists, speculators would feature prominently.

Speculators are those who buy or sell in the hope of profiting from subsequent price changes. Typically they will buy cheap in the hope of selling at a higher price later, or sell goods they do not have, hoping to buy those goods at a lower price when the time comes for them to deliver.

A very common type of speculation involves trading in *futures*. A dealer will agree a price now for goods to be delivered in the future, hoping that the price of those goods will change in his or her favour later on. A speculator might agree a price in the spring on a harvest to be delivered in the autumn. He or she estimates what the crop might be worth at the time it is harvested, taking into account such factors as the weather, the likely demand, and whether or not the harvest will be a big one. If they estimated correctly, and luck is on their side as well, they will be able to sell the harvest for more than they paid in advance for it. If circumstance and fortune go against them, they will lose money. But for either outcome the farmer is secure in the price that was agreed in the spring.

Another common speculative activity sees people trading in currency futures, buying and selling currencies now for delivery in the future, and hoping to make money on changes in their value between now and then. In cases such as these the activity seems to outsiders to be little more than gambling, similar to betting on the outcome of the spin of a roulette wheel.

It is not quite that simple, though, in that for honest roulette tables the outcome depends on pure chance, whereas in the futures markets one can estimate how some of the factors that bear on price might turn out. The skilled speculator uses judgement to calculate how likely prices are to rise or fall. Even if it calls for skill and judgement, though, the question is still, 'Does it do anything useful?'

While people might be persuaded to recognise the value of convenience added by middle-men, few can see any value added by speculators. The truth is that speculators actually do add value, although it is even less visible than that of convenience, and much less readily understood by outsiders. They add the value of security.

Managing risk

What speculators actually do is manage risk. Life is uncertain, and many people prefer the certainty of a fixed and assured price rather than a possible future one which might be higher, but might leave them impoverished. Farmers often like to know what price their harvest will fetch because they need to plan and to buy equipment and seed.

Speculators buy futures which offer that certainty. They have to be highly skilled at predicting likely outcomes, and prepared to carry that risk. In doing so they smooth out the risks for others. The speculator, by offering a fixed price now, takes on the uncertainty with its possibilities of gain, and removes the uncertainty from others less well placed or equipped to handle it.

The speculator is prepared to carry the occasional losses in a way that a farmer, for example, might not be able to do. Speculators take their chances, balancing gains against losses, and using their skill and judgement to end up ahead on average.

A businessman buying goods from abroad does not know what value in his own currency he might have to pay. Nor does an exporter know what currency variations might do to his prices by the time he is paid. In both cases they might, like the farmer, prefer to reduce the risks they are exposed to by agreeing a price now for the currency they will need later. It brings security to a deal that would otherwise be fraught with uncertainty. The risks are still there, but now they are carried by a professional risk-taker, the speculator who does this for a living.

Those who settle early for a fixed price are sometimes dismayed to see the speculator who promised them that price making money that could have been theirs. Some of them resent the fact that the speculator did no work to produce those goods. He or she came in at a late stage and made their profit through a simple transaction, unlike the producer who toiled to produce the goods.

The value added by the speculator includes time and risk. Other things being equal, something to be enjoyed now is worth more than it is in the future. The enjoyment it makes possible in the intervening time adds to its value, together with the certainty of present enjoyment compared with the risk that the future enjoyment might not happen. Although these factors are invisible, they nonetheless add value. The speculator who buys futures takes not only the goods, but the delay in taking delivery of them, plus the risk of a substantial fall in their value by the time this happens.

Far from being mere parasites who make money by gambling on uncertain outcomes, speculators provide a valued service by taking risk from those ill-equipped or unprepared to handle it. They add security, and give others the ability to plan confidently in an uncertain world. This is a valuable and marketable skill, one which oils the wheels of commerce; this is why they are paid for exercising it.

ENTERPRISE

President George W. Bush was mocked for his sometimes tortuous and folksy use of language. In a famous quote attributed to him he allegedly exclaimed that "the French have no word for entrepreneur". The humour derives from the fact that 'entrepreneur' is a French word. Nonetheless, President Bush could have been right on this occasion because the French use 'entrepreneur' where we might use 'tradesman'. It refers to people who provide skilled or semi-skilled services such as plumbers and window-fitters, whereas the English use of the word carries with it the idea of an economic innovator or pioneer, perhaps someone who sets up a new business.

MOST PEOPLE FIT into an economy by doing something that others do in established ways. They settle into a recognisable niche, providing goods and services that others provide in a similar fashion. Most people do this by taking a job with a firm, contributing to the output of the firm as they are directed to, and being paid a wage or salary in return. They add value to the goods or services whose output they contribute to, and are paid out of that increased value.

Entrepreneurs are different, in that they bring something new to the economy. They are people who spot a market opportunity and seek to take advantage of it.

They see how particular goods and services might be improved and made more valuable to customers. Sometimes this might be by improvements in the quality, enabling the goods and services to provide greater satisfaction to customers. Sometimes it might be efficiencies in production that enable goods to be made more cheaply and sold at lower prices. Less often, but more dramatically, they might bring completely new products onto the market, products previously unobtainable, but ones they think people will be ready to buy.

Whatever it is, it represents something new on the market, and the entrepreneurs hope that people will buy the new product or service in preference to those they were buying before. They want to capture market share, with people spending enough on the new offering to generate profits that will come their way.

In anticipation of those future returns, the entrepreneur commits both time and resources to the development of their innovation, and to the steps it takes to bring it to the point where it can be offered for sale. The entrepreneur needs money to set up that process, and will probably need labour to help produce it. The name entrepreneur is said to derive from the fact that he or she stands between capital and labour and brings them together in an enterprise. Very often some equipment will be needed, either machinery or tools, and there will often be a requirement for premises and raw materials.

All of this takes money, so the entrepreneur has to raise capital. Many of them put up their own savings, and accept backing from their family and friends. When this proves insufficient, they have to raise outside finance by borrowing money at interest.

Hoping for success

The whole activity is full of risk. The entrepreneur is taking a huge gamble that the new product or process will find sufficient favour with the public that they will buy it, and at a price which will make the whole activity worthwhile. The money paid by consumers at the end has to pay for the costs of production, including labour, raw materials and rent of premises. It has to cover the cost of the funds borrowed to undertake the activity, and there has to be enough to justify the time and effort that it took on the part of the entrepreneur, and the risk that accompanied it.

Most entrepreneurs find that things rarely go as smoothly in practice as they envisaged in the original business plan. Things go wrong unexpectedly; there are unforeseen crises; emergencies have to be addressed; problems occur during production and marketing. It is, to put it mildly, a risky and stressful activity. Instead of undertaking so bold and hazardous a venture, the entrepreneur could have opted for a safe and comfortable life as a salaried employee of a company, letting someone else take the risks and carry the burdens and the consequences.

Why, then, do people do it? The answers are varied. In the first place, there are fortunes to be made. The entrepreneur who successfully brings a new product or process to market, and finds there is a ready demand for it, can make substantial amounts of money. Since the idea is new it can sell, initially at least, with little if any competition. Entrepreneurs who get it right can find the business they establish growing into a successful corporation, perhaps ultimately worth millions of pounds.

Of course, the potential riches which success might bring have to be balanced against the losses that are risked by engaging in the enterprise. But the allure of wealth is part of the process by which every person seeks to better their condition, and for many it is a sufficient incentive to justify taking the risk.

When entrepreneurs are interviewed or have their life stories written up, as successful ones do, many say that money is not the main motivation. While it is a goal, and is for most people the measure of success, many cite the achievement itself as a stronger motivation. It is for them the thrill of achievement, the creation of something new and important, that brings more satisfaction to them than the money that accompanies it. This is a feeling which many athletes recognise: that winning the contest matters more than the prize or the reward that go with the victory. It is the sense of personal achievement, of being responsible for building something worthwhile.

Yet another class of entrepreneurs say that it is not the money, or even the achievement itself, which motivates them. Some point instead to the excitement of the activity, deriving their pleasure as hunters do, from the thrills of the chase. To such people entrepreneurial activity offers the chance to do something exciting and risky, to take part in a contest where there are some winners and many losers, and to test their mettle against others similarly engaged.

There is no doubt, listening to what entrepreneurs say, that it can be a very thrilling activity. As they go through the process of surmounting successive crises and resolving the problems that crop up along their way, many derive satisfaction from the game itself, rather than from the result gained at the end of it. Many describe the early days of their enterprise as stressful ones filled with worry. Many tell how they lost sleep and lost weight in coping with cash shortages, near-insolvency, and the need to meet well-nigh unattainable commitments within impossible time frames. Yet they usually tell such stories with relish, recapturing the excitement that the experience brought them, and thrilling again to the trials they went through.

Whether they do it for the money, the desire to create something worthwhile, or for the thrill of the activity itself, entrepreneurs constitute a very dynamic part of the economic process. They are the ones who keep it moving forward into new areas, ever seeking to improve value, to use resources more efficiently, and to extend the range of products and processes that increase life's comforts, conveniences and opportunities.

Sharing the risk

The risks and the costs of entrepreneurship are so great that they sometimes lie beyond the reach of single individuals, which is why people have found various ways in which they can be shared between several participants.

Co-operative ventures have existed for hundreds, perhaps thousands, of years. One of the early types involved merchants joining together to kit out and crew a ship for what was hoped would be a profitable voyage. A group would provide between them the funds needed for the enterprise. If the voyage were successful, returning a profitable cargo, the proceeds would be shared out between the merchants in proportion to the investment each had made in the enterprise. Should the ship be lost, then each lost what they had put in, with no single individual having to carry the entire loss.

The successors of such joint enterprises were companies formed by partners, each contributing a share. If the company prospered in its trading, the partners divided the profits between them in proportion to their various share holdings. The shares they held could be bought and sold, so outsiders could buy a stake in a company by buying shares from one or more of the partners.

In essence this is how many modern companies work. Buying shares in them means buying a proportion of the company, carrying with it the entitlement to a share of any profits it makes. When profits are distributed, they go to shareholders in proportion to the number of shares that they own. The distribution of profits, which is called a dividend, is often done annually, and represents income for the shareholder on the investment they made by buying the shares.

There is another way in which shareholders can make money from their investment. The price of the shares they bought goes up or down, depending on how well the company is doing. A successful company making good profits will usually attract more potential buyers for its shares, generally causing them to rise in price. This means that shareholder, in addition to the dividends paid out of the company's profits, might also find their shares are now themselves worth more. If the shareholder is able to sell the shares at a higher price than they paid for them, they make a capital gain as well as any dividend payments they received while holding their shares.

Historically, over the long term, investors have tended to secure higher returns by putting their money into company shares than by lending it out at interest. The combination of dividend payments and capital appreciation in the value of their shares has historically been higher than interest rates available over the same period of time.

Running a business partnership

When a handful of people join together in a venture, each contributing funds and buying a share of the enterprise, it is relatively easy for them to agree on how it should be run and what activities it should undertake. Even with small numbers there might be disagreements, but it is comparatively easy for decisions to be taken. The general rule is that those with the greatest share have the greatest say. If those representing one point of view have with them people owning more than half the investment, they will generally prevail over those holding only a minority share. It is rather like a democracy, but instead of each individual having one vote, each shareholder has votes in proportion to their share.

As enterprises become larger and involve many more shareholders, the decision-making process inevitably becomes more formalised. Since hundreds or thousands of owners can hardly meet together every day to take decisions, they delegate that power by electing a board of directors to take the day-to-day decisions about how the company shall be run. This is somewhat similar to electing a representative in a democratic government. Since we cannot all meet every day in the city square to vote on policy, as citizens of ancient Athens did, we choose representatives to do this on our behalf. A similar process is used with companies.

The directors of a company are ultimately answerable to the shareholders. Those who own shares vote in proportion to the size of their holding. They appoint directors and can dismiss them. Some analysts claim that ordinary shareholders have too little power in modern companies, and that the interests of the directors can be separate from those of the shareholders. Big investment funds can hold a large percentage of the shares of a company, and a few of them acting in concert can exercise a power that is well beyond any that an ordinary shareholder can aspire to. Nonetheless, the shareholders collectively have the chance to ratify or overturn the decisions made by their directors.

In a gripping scene in the movie *Wall Street* (1987; dir. Oliver Stone), the corporate raider, Gordon Gecko, confronts the company's board at the annual shareholder meeting, criticising the way the directors have behaved, and appealing to the ordinary shareholders to dismiss them and accept his own vision of the company's future. It is a real-life possibility, albeit a rare one. In general it takes considerable malpractice to motivate the shareholders of a company to over-rule or throw out the directors their vote has appointed. As with most company activity, there are fewer complaints when things are going well than when they go badly.

When good business is being done, profits being made, and good dividends are being paid to share-owners, criticism of the board will usually be more mute than when losses are made and shareholders are not receiving an adequate return for the funds they have invested. It is very similar in a democracy, in that governments that preside over prosperity are more likely to be popular and to be re-elected than those which preside over economic downturns and privation.

Profit is the purpose

Profit lies at the heart of business, for this is the purpose of the activity. Money is invested and put at risk, and present enjoyment is deferred. It is done in the hope that greater wealth will be generated. That means that customers will choose to buy the goods and services produced, that profits will be made, and that dividends will be distributed to those who invested.

Profit is an important lynchpin of economic growth. If profits are being made, people will set aside present consumption and invest funds for future gain. This boosts the total invested in the production of goods and services, and increases the efficiency of that production. The net result is an increase in the wealth of society. It is by processes such as these that the developed nations of the world accumulated their stock of capital and raised their standard of living.

For successful enterprises, profit is the justification for the risk and commitment that their investors make. But what about the ones which fail to make profits? The answer is that they usually disband or are restructured, with any remaining capital redeployed to where it might be used with more success. Those who invested in unsuccessful businesses lose money. The losses are the downside of the risk they took to make gains.

Limited liability

In the mid-19th century, legislation was enacted limiting the amount to which investors stood at risk. Normally this is the amount they have invested in a particular enterprise, rather than any additional wealth they might have independent of that.

If, for example, a company fails, leaving many debts, the investors in that company stand to lose what they have invested in it, but no more. Their personal wealth is not at risk to those seeking to recover money they are owed. This is called 'limited liability', and makes it possible for enterprises to fail without bankrupting those who invested in them. Usually they lose some or all of their investment, and no more than that.

Limited liability was controversial when it was introduced, and has its critics even today. It is certainly true that enterprise would be a far riskier activity without it, and people would be much less ready to invest. Someone might buy shares in a company hoping to receive dividends and capital gains. Most people do so in the knowledge that some companies can fail, just as some succeed, and they might lose money on the enterprise. They would be less keen to buy if their entire wealth was at stake, and they were liable for any debts the company found itself unable to pay. The knowledge that their bank account could be emptied, and their house and property sold to meet a company's debts, would lead many people to seek other ways of making money.

If there were no limited liability, life would be particularly difficult for new enterprises which carry with them the additional risk of the unknown. Life is uncertain, and many new businesses fail. Many of those who invest in them often do so in the knowledge that they could fail, hoping that the ones that do succeed will bring sufficiently handsome returns to make up for the losses on those that fail. Limited liability means that investors stand to lose no more than the amount they have put at risk. On the other hand, those who lend money to limited liability companies know this, and can be less ready to lend without collateral or guarantees.

Dividends

While people might have other reasons for buying shares in a company, the prime motivation is to make money. The investor buys shares, and with them a proportion of the company and a stake in its activities. He or she hopes that the value of their investment will be secure, but they also hope that the profits made by the company will be distributed to shareholders as dividends, bringing a return on the money they invested.

It is another part of the activity of foregoing present enjoyment in return for greater future rewards. Successful companies make profits. Some of that they keep as assets, either as reserves set aside for possible emergencies, or as a capital pool to fund business expansion and new activities that could make even more money in the future.

Some of it will, however, be distributed, handed out to the shareholders in proportion to their holding, and it is this return over the years that boosts shareholders' wealth and justifies their investment.

Appreciation

Capital gain adds to that process. In addition to the dividends they receive, shareholders gain from any rises in the market value of their shares. If the company makes more profits, its shares become attractive to other investors prepared to pay a little more for them, and the price of the shares rises on the stock markets. The investor who bought some a while back can now sell for a higher price than he or she paid, adding this gain to the dividends they have received while they held the shares.

This has been a major factor in the growth of capital and the accumulation of wealth. Over the long term of perhaps 150 years, the UK economy has grown at an average of roughly 1.5 per cent each year. Other advanced economies have also grown steadily in the long term, not excluding the occasional downturn and depression. This steady economic growth reflects a steady increase in the amount of business activity, and in the profits and value of companies. There has scarce been a better long-term investment than in equities (shares in business).

Of course shares in individual companies might rise or fall. Some might rise spectacularly, and others lose their value altogether. But taking the market as a whole, which people can do by diversifying their share-holding across many different companies, investors have been able to secure these steady gains in the average worth of their holdings.

This factor, no less than the dividends paid on shares, has made the stock market a place where investors have been able to secure steady increases in the value of the investment they put in.

Investment funds, which invest money on behalf of their clients, have long known this, and have usually made sure that they have a fair spread of their investment portfolio in company shares. Many of them balance this by holding some of their investment in bonds as well. Bonds issued by governments at a guaranteed interest are somewhat safer than equities, but in the long term they tend to make lower returns.

MONEY
AND CURRENCY

Barter involves the trade of goods or services for other goods or services. It is how exchange began, but it survives into modern times, often when people have nothing but goods to trade. In *To Kill a Mockingbird* (1960, by Harper Lee), the lawyer Atticus Finch accepts farm produce from Mr Cunningham in exchange for his services. Children do it routinely with toys and collector's cards. One recent case gained worldwide attention:

"My name is Kyle MacDonald and I traded one red paperclip for a house. I started with one red paperclip on July 12, 2005 and 14 trades later, on July 12, 2006 I traded with the Town of Kipling, Saskatchewan for a house located at 503 Main Street." (**oneredpaperclip.blogspot.com**)

IT MIGHT BE EASY in any individual transaction to calculate how much of one item can be traded for another. It depends on how much the parties value the different items. In the story of the old man catching fish with his cormorant, he was prepared to trade his six fish for a large bag of rice, but not for a small one.

When the baker needs a new pair of shoes, he might bargain with the cobbler about the number of loaves of bread he has to hand over in order to buy them. It might take 20 loaves to buy a pair of shoes, and here we encounter one of the problems of exchange. The cobbler probably does not want 20 loaves of bread. Bread is a perishable commodity, much more so than shoes. His small family might get through one loaf a day, so most of the 20 loaves will have gone stale before he wants to eat them.

What the cobbler can do, of course, is take 20 loaves in exchange for the shoes he has made, and then rush off to trade maybe 18 of them for things he does need. He has to do this quickly because the bread will not stay fresh. The demand is not for bread; it is for fresh bread. The cobbler might find that the candle-maker needs two loaves, the dressmaker another two, and so on, thus buying in needed supplies in return for the 18 loaves he does not need himself.

This is very cumbersome, time-consuming, and exposed to the vicissitudes of fortune. He has to find all of the people prepared to take payment in loaves for their produce, agree a rate of exchange, and complete all of the transactions while the bread remains fresh.

The cobbler has another option, though. He can go to a market stallholder, a middle-man like the one who gave the fisherman rice in exchange for his six fish. The stallholder might give the cobbler a variety of goods he does want in return for the 18 loaves he does not. If he is a good stallholder who knows what he is doing, he will know whether or not he can exchange those loaves to customers who want them while the bread is still fresh enough to be tradable.

From the cobbler's point of view this is a more satisfactory procedure, in that it saves him the trouble of finding different people to take the bread. He knows he might receive a lower rate of exchange for the bread, in that the middle-man has to take his cut, but this is compensated for by the convenience and the removal of risk.

This is a better option for the cobbler than trying to move the loaves he does not want on to customers who do want them, but it still has many of the disadvantages of a barter economy. If goods are to be traded for other goods, those who have them must be matched up with those who want them.

This might be cumbersome enough without the added difficulty that some goods are perishable. The match-making must be done while the goods are still sufficiently fresh to have value. This lends an urgency to the task and brings with it the risk that a match might not be completed while the goods are still fresh.

The item to introduce into this activity is some non-perishable item which everyone is prepared to accept – a universal medium of exchange. This is where money enters the equation. In the exchanges started by the fisherman, only one was a barter deal. The fish were exchanged for rice, but the other deals involved money. The fish were sold on to the restaurateur for cash, and then to the diners for cash. It is worth noting, too, that only the fish were immediately perishable; they go bad quickly. The rice, properly stored, lasts a lot longer, as does the money itself.

Money factors in time

One of the main advantages of money is that it factors time into exchanges. We do not all need our wants to be satisfied on the same day. The cobbler would much rather have money from the baker instead of bread loaves in return for the shoes he has made. Because money lasts and is universally accepted, he does not need to find buyers on the same day, as he would for the 18 spare bread loaves.

It is one of the major advantages of money that it lasts. People do not need to circulate it before it loses value; instead it can be used as a store of value. It must also be widely acceptable. The cobbler will only accept money from the baker for his shoes if he knows that others will accept the money for the goods he himself might want.

Originally money took the form of commodities that were widely acceptable because they were sufficiently rare and most people wanted them. Gold and silver were desired for their use in jewellery and decoration. This and their rarity made them an acceptable medium of exchange. They held their value, did not degrade significantly over time, and were widely accepted. This meant that even people who did not actually want gold and silver for ornamental purposes could want these precious metals to exchange for the things they did desire.

When we look at what it is that makes something acceptable as money, one element that keeps appearing is confidence. People must be sure that it will be accepted by others as a medium of exchange. Different things have been used as money at different times and in different cultures, but all of them have been things in which people had confidence. People believed that they would hold their value, and that others would accept them in turn. Cowrie shells at one stage have been used as money; they held their value and were widely accepted.

The Romans sometimes paid the soldiers of their legions with salt. It was acceptable because it had a value in preserving and adding flavour to food. It could be divided up and weighed, and was readily transportable. If kept well, it could hold its value without degrading. A soldier could trade the salt he received for other items that he wanted, knowing it would be acceptable as payment.

Some of our modern expressions come from this practice. We speak of someone being 'worth his salt', meaning that he merits his wages, and the modern word 'salary' is derived from the Latin word for salt.

Qualities suitable for money

It helps if whatever is used as money can be divided up into convenient units, so that it can be used as a measure of value, comparing the value of different items by contrasting the different units of money each can command. Gold and silver were issued in denominations of particular weight, and issued in bars and coins with the value stamped upon them.

Money should also be fungible, meaning that any unit of it is no different from any equal unit. An ounce of gold or silver is the same as any other ounce of gold or silver. One unit of money can stand in for any similar unit. This is one reason why diamonds are not as useful a form of currency as gold and silver. Diamonds differ from one another, and are of different qualities, whereas measures of gold and silver of equal purity do not.

Confidence in money is what makes it acceptable, and this includes the confidence that it has not been tampered with to undermine its value. People want to be assured that the coin circulating as an ounce of gold or silver does indeed contain precisely that amount of the precious metal, and has not been diluted by having baser metals mixed with it, or diminished by having small amounts of the metal shaved from the edges.

The practice of shaving or clipping coinage to degrade its value is one reason why we often find coins with rilled edges, or with inscriptions around the edge, so that people can see if they have been tampered with.

If some coins were diluted with baser metals, word travelled fast, and coins from that source would command less confidence, and be worth less than their face value. Reputation was the key. An impeccably honest source whose currency was reliable was the money of choice because people knew they could rely on it.

Bullion coins have been issued from many sources, and are still being issued today. One renowned for its quality was the silver coinage originally minted by the Counts of Schlick in Joachimsthal, Bohemia, meaning Joachim's valley. The widely-respected coins were called 'Joachimsthalers,' abbreviated to thalers (pronounced 'tah-lers') and were widely accepted, not only across Europe, but in the New World city of New Amsterdam, which later became New York. When the new United States came to adopt a currency, the units took their name from these 'thalers', which became 'dollars'.

Notes as receipts

The practice developed of people being given receipts for amounts of gold deposited at banks, and the receipts themselves were traded as substitutes for the real thing. They were literally 'as good as gold', and accepted as its equivalent. This was one of the main origins of paper money, since the receipts were convenient and highly portable. Originally they represented drawing rights on deposited bullion.

Although the notes could theoretically be exchanged for the gold or silver they represented, such exchange was discouraged. The old Sterling pound note bore the legend, "Promise to pay the bearer on demand the sum of one pound", but if you had taken one to a bank, they would have only given you another one in exchange to redeem that promise.

This was not of great consequence so long as the notes each represented a specific amount of gold on deposit somewhere. People could have confidence that the notes would hold their value because they had confidence that the gold they represented would hold its value. In the 20th century, however, governments abandoned the so-called 'gold standard' and issued what was called 'fiat currency'. *Fiat* is a Latin word meaning 'let it be done', and the currency was supposed to have value simply because the government said it did. People accepted the notes because they believed the government would maintain their value, and would back that promise with tax revenues.

Nearly all modern currencies are fiat ones, imposed and backed by governments. One feature of this is that governments are not limited by the quantity of bullion at their disposal. They can issue the currency they think their economies need, without depending on supplies of gold and silver stored somewhere to back it with. There is another side to this, in that governments are no longer restrained in their issuing of notes by the need to back them with precious metals. Governments could theoretically issue as much currency as they wished, as some have done with disastrous consequences.

The problem is that people want money, as they want other things. They want money for its convenience, to store value as savings, and to exchange it for things they need on a daily basis. As with other commodities, the price of money relative to other goods will vary according to how much of it people want, and how much is available. If the government floods the market with newly-printed money, the surplus of the supply of it over the demand will see a fall in its price measured against other goods. There will be too much money chasing the available goods, and prices will rise.

Too much money

This is basically what inflation is about. It happens when government increases the money supply such that it outstrips any increases in production. Barring unusual circumstances, the result is a general rise in prices as money loses its value.

But why should government increase the supply of money like this? The answer is that it wants to spend, and hesitates to raise the money for this by more orthodox means. In wartime, governments want to spend on troops and armaments. In peacetime, they want to spend on social programmes that attract voters. In both cases they need money, and in both they find this difficult to raise through taxation. Basically they want to spend more money than taxpayers will willingly part with. Governments which try to fund programmes like this by taxation find that their electorates reject the proposed taxes and vote for other parties instead.

There are three principal ways in which governments acquire money. They can raise it through taxation, they can borrow it, or they can print it. There is technically a fourth way, in which they can raise money by selling things. They can sell land, perhaps, or parts of the electromagnetic spectrum they have claimed ownership of. Or they can sell things the government has acquired in the past, such as state industries and other assets.

The problem for government is that these are one-offs. Once sold, they cannot be sold again. They cannot therefore finance programmes that need regular annual expenditure, or the government will need to find other things to sell in the following year and in the year after that, and will eventually run out.

Taxation is unpopular with taxpayers; borrowing only postpones the problem because the money will have to be repaid at some stage. This leaves inflation as the easiest option. By printing extra money the government dilutes the value of everyone else's money, so it amounts to a form of invisible taxation. It is an easier option than ordinary taxation because it is relatively surreptitious. People do not always associate the higher prices they have to pay with government profligacy.

Because of its political attractions, inflation has been inflicted on most countries over the past century and a half. Money in most of them will buy only a fraction of what it did just a few decades ago. Most of their citizens listen with amazement as their grandparents tell stories of the prices that prevailed in their youth. For that matter, those grandparents look with equal amazement at the salaries earned by their grandchildren.

Hyper-inflation

The remorseless government inflation of money has reduced its buying power almost everywhere. In a few cases of hyper-inflation it has brought about total collapse of a currency, and even of an economy. The example usually quoted is the inflation of the Weimar Republic which followed Germany's defeat in World War I. It eventually took barrow-loads of banknotes to buy groceries, and Reichmark notes were regularly over-stamped with many zeros added to denote they now represented millions of marks instead of mere tens or hundreds.

In more recent times there has been the example of Zimbabwe, where the government financed its activity by printing Zimbabwe dollars as the economy collapsed. Soon notes were being issued in billions, and eventually trillions, of dollars, but it still took several of them to buy basic foodstuffs like bread. There were stories of banknotes being used as toilet paper, since they were worth less than the real article. By an accident of history, the Zimbabwe notes were actually minted by the same company which many decades earlier had printed the banknotes of the Weimar Republic.

It seems unlikely that people would ever accept payment in such worthless currencies, but the truth is that almost always they are forced to do so by their government. Most governments enact a monopoly over money. They reserve the sole right to issue it, and to dictate what shall and shall not be acceptable. Under so-called 'legal tender' laws, governments insist that payment in their own currency has to be accepted, and in many cases make it illegal for other currencies to be used in trading.

When 'good' money which has kept its value trades alongside money that has been devalued by inflation, people tend to save the 'good' money and only make payments in the degraded currency. This is called Gresham's Law, and expresses the fact that 'bad money drives out good'. In the Middle Ages people tried to pay with the clipped or diluted coins, and to save any unadulterated coins for themselves.

It should be noted, though, that this only operates where 'legal tender' mandates acceptance of the inferior money. In the absence of such compulsion, people normally choose to accept only the honest money, reversing Gresham's Law and replacing it by a rule that 'good money drives out bad'.

As well as eroding the value of savings, inflation makes investment difficult because investment is about the future, and people find it difficult to predict what things will be worth and what prices will be like by the time any new production comes on line.

Debtors benefit

Inflation has its beneficiaries, which notably include debtors. Since money is losing value, any debts will be worth less in real terms. Their value, measured against the goods and services they could buy, decreases over time when there is inflation, which makes them easier to repay. Of course creditors lose out because when they are repaid, the money they receive back, even with interest added, has less buying power than the money they lent out.

The debtors who benefit from inflation nearly always include governments, because most governments carry a burden of debt. Inflating their currency is a way of paying their creditors with money that buys less than it did when they were lent it.

People used to think that unemployed people benefited from inflation. The supposition was that when extra money was printed and put into circulation, people felt richer and spent more. The extra demand was supposed to create more jobs. For a time it seemed to work, and people thought there was a direct relationship between inflation and unemployment, called the Phillips Curve after the New Zealand economist, William Phillips, who developed it.

Its spurious nature was revealed once people realised that the extra money was illusory, created by diluting the value of everyone else's money. Rather than being a source of real demand, the new money simply reduced demand elsewhere as people's existing money would buy less.

Some economists suggested that inflation could be used to mitigate the ups and downs of the economy. If government printed extra money during an economic downturn, it was supposed that the extra demand it created would counter the slow-down and keep people in jobs they might otherwise have lost.

What inflation does

This was, and still is, a very controversial subject. The new money created by government does not suddenly spread itself evenly over the whole economy. It comes from government and spreads out from there. Its chief effect is to make investment seem more attractive than it really is, once the fall in the value of money is accounted for.

People see how available money is, thanks to the new supply, and make erroneous decisions about people's buying power. They invest in more production, only to find when it comes on line that people are not spending more. Instead they are finding that their money buys less than it did. One result is that some of those who were taken into employment as part of the expansion, now find themselves out of jobs when the anticipated demand fails to materialise.

Inflation still remains a very controversial subject, not least because it redistributes wealth from one part of the population in order to benefit another. It benefits debtors, who usually include governments, but it robs savers of the value of what they have put aside. In many modern economies it is older people who tend to hold many of the savings and assets which are devalued by inflation, and who thus suffer its consequences most keenly.

It also deprives investors and those who lend money of the value they hoped to gain by putting their money to work, and discourages others from doing so. This, in turn, hits society's ability to generate new wealth in the future, and with it new jobs.

Most people, given a choice, would rather trade in honest money that kept its value, and it is a misfortune of modern societies that governments have the ability to thwart that desire, and regularly choose to do so.

BANKS AND FINANCE

In a 1970s' television commercial for a small town bank, a customer walked into the bank and confronted the manager.

"I want to make sure that my money is safe," demanded the customer. "Can I see it?"

"Of course," replied the manager with a smile. "Follow me."

He led the customer to the vault, twiddled the knobs of the combination, and swung open the huge, thick circular door. Beyond it lay not the expected vault packed with banknotes and perhaps gold bars. It led instead into the High Street.

The manager helped the customer through the door and into the street.

"See here," he said, pointing to a hairdresser's. "When Joe needed to expand his barber's shop, we lent him the money to fit out an extra room. And here, when Ellen wanted to extend her diner to add extra tables, we put up the money she needed."

The manager showed him other local businesses that had been similarly helped, then turned to the surprised customer and said, "So you see, your money is quite safe. It's working for the community."

IT MIGHT HAVE ONLY been a TV commercial, but it expressed an important truth, one largely misunderstood by the general public. Banks do indeed have vaults, but they are largely used temporarily for money in transit, rather than for the safe storage of customer deposits. The money was stored instead in the High Street businesses to which it had been lent.

Banks are middle-men who deal in money. Other middle-men bring suppliers and customers together for items such as groceries or tailoring or kitchen appliances, but bankers do it with money. Their function is to act as go-betweens for those who want to invest money and those who want to borrow money.

Banks serve a highly necessary function, and have been with us a long time. Some forms of them are known to have been present in the ancient Persian and Phoenician empires. Their modern form seems to have started in the mediaeval Italian city states, where financiers sat alongside one another on a bench, called a *banco*, to transact lending and money-changing. The word may be derived from the older Roman word, *bancu*, giving a long heritage to sitting on benches to talk about money. People doing business have long needed money, and the bank was where they went to obtain it.

The bank is a business; its primary purpose is to make money. Like other middle-men, it does this by providing a convenience that customers think worth paying for. In ordinary High Street banking, called retail banking, the depositors want somewhere to put their money where it will earn something for them, but be safe while it is doing so. Those who want to earn higher returns, and are prepared to take the greater risks that usually accompany the prospect of doing so, go somewhere else; the High Street bank is not generally for them, even though some may offer specialist services to cater for that minority market.

The amount of interest banks pay depends on market conditions such as the general availability of money and the rate the bank itself has to pay for it. It can also vary with the general state of the economy. In particular the rate offered to depositors depends on the degree of accessibility demanded. If a customer wants to be able to draw out their money at any time without notice, the interest rate will be lower than for a customer prepared to give three months' notice of a withdrawal. The reason is that the bank itself has more uses for longer-term funds.

Banks need to keep a certain level of liquidity – access to cash – to meet the withdrawal demands their customers are likely to make. Since they lend it out, rather than storing it in their vaults, most of it is being used at any one time. The bank has to estimate the likely level of withdrawals, and secure enough cash in hand to meet them.

Fractional reserve banking

When banknotes were promises secured by gold bullion, those holding the bullion found that as the notes were circulated or stored, the bullion they represented was not all redeemed at once. They could therefore use some of it to invest themselves in interest-bearing bonds.

Banks do something similar today. Knowing that their depositors will not all return at once to claim their money back, the bank will lend out large amounts of it, only keeping enough readily available to meet likely demand. This has the effect of increasing the amount of money moving around the economy, and makes a great deal more available to business than would be there otherwise. Small savers do not know enough about business opportunities and risks, so the bank is able to put their money to work on their behalf.

This kind of reserve banking puts more money into circulation, but is not without its risks. It depends to some extent on how conservative the bank has been in its lending. Banks have to weigh up how risky their lending is, and not put too much of their depositors' cash into deals that might fail.

If an economic downturn is accompanied by failures in key sectors the bank has lent money to, there is the risk that people might default on the debts they owe it, perhaps leaving the bank with insufficient short-term cash to meet likely withdrawals.

During the 2008 banking crisis, one factor identified was the over-exposure of some banks to high-risk debtors in the housing market. Some mortgages carried a high risk of default, but by the time they had been bundled together in packages that could be sold, traded, and invested in, most people did not appreciate the high risk of default they carried. Banks which held significant numbers of such debtors on their books found themselves dangerously short of the reserves they needed to meet their own obligations.

When people lose confidence

The worst thing that can happen to a bank is for depositors to demand more of their money than the bank can supply at that point. This might happen if people lose confidence in their bank, and feel their funds might no longer be safe. At such times they hurry to withdraw their deposits in case the bank fails, and in doing so make that event much more likely to happen.

In the very worst cases there is what is called a 'run' on the bank as queues of anxious depositors line up to withdraw their money while they still can, and the bank struggles to find sufficient funds to meet the demand, bearing in mind that many of their funds are tied up in long-term loans to businesses.

In practice many governments are not prepared to allow High Street retail banks to fail and cause their depositors to lose their savings. Governments do not want their citizens to suffer because of mismanagement or misjudgement on the part of banks, and tend to step in on such occasions to bail out the banks concerned, or even take them into state ownership for a time. Politicians fear the wrath of aggrieved depositors if they fail to protect them.

Less concern is shown for the fate of commercial banks which chiefly specialise in providing banking services to corporations. These operate largely in the world of business, which is assumed to have its risks and to be capable of dealing with them. There is less public concern over corporations that lose money than is shown for ordinary citizens in a similar position.

Investment banking

Still further removed from the general public are the investment banks which engage in their own trades, buying and selling stocks and bonds in order to generate profits. Sometimes they will guarantee new issues of shares or bonds, making money if their prices go up, and exposing themselves to losses if they go down. Such banks will often form associations with individual companies, advising them and assisting them in market activities such as the takeover of other firms.

These activities carry much higher risks than those which retail banks engage in. They carry the chances of huge profits, but also of mind-boggling losses. This is something which high-rolling professionals might feel comfortable with, but these are not activities that most governments would want their ordinary citizens exposed to.

The astronomical salaries and especially bonuses to be seen in the world of investment banking are far removed from the more humdrum, but highly necessary, work of retail banks in taking in deposits and making loans available. The rewards there are more modest, in accordance with the lower levels of risk. Some might say, too, that the skill required of a local bank manager is not on the same level as that of a high-rolling market maker who can trade hundreds of millions in a second.

What the local bank manager has to do is judge which businesses and potential businesses are worth lending money to, balancing the risks against the likely rewards. They have to assess which proposed businesses might merit a loan, and what kind of security should be demanded against it. They have to charge interest on their loan in such a way that those who prosper and repay their loans with interest outweigh those who fail to make the grade and cannot repay the bank.

Private banks, even local ones, have in the past issued their own notes, backed by their own resources and their reputation. As with all money, confidence is the major part of its acceptability.

In most modern economies the government has established a monopoly of the issuing of currency, and does so through a central bank, sometimes called a national bank. Even where individual banks are still allowed to issue notes, it is almost universal for the central bank to require them to deposit funds with which to back them.

In practice this removes the private bank's freedom to issue its own currency, even if it continues to print its own banknotes. There are still banknotes issued by different Scottish banks, but they can no longer do so independently of the Bank of England.

Central bank

The central bank is charged with control of the nation's currency. It sets the interest rate it charges other banks for money, which in turn affects the rate they can charge their own customers. The central bank attempts to control, by that interest rate, the availability of credit and the amount of money circulating in the economy.

It is a somewhat crude instrument, rather than one which can be fine-tuned with precision. In practice there are influences, many of them originating from abroad, which are beyond the control of any one central bank.

The central banks of the USA and Britain have slightly different missions. The Bank of England has been independent of the UK government since 1997, although its key personnel are still appointed by the Chancellor of the Exchequer. It is charged with keeping inflation to a target of 2 per cent. If it falls more than a percentage point above or below that figure, the Governor of the Bank has to write to the Chancellor explaining what happened and what is to be done about it. The figure of 2 per cent is close to Britain's historic long-term growth rate, and represents the government's desire to keep prices stable. Average prices tend to be steady when the inflation rate coincides with the long-term growth rate.

The Federal Reserve Board in the USA is similarly charged with controlling inflation, but is given the extra duty of sustaining the economy. If the US economy dips dramatically, the Fed is expected to take corrective action.

In practice, although their nominal roles are somewhat different, many analysts reckon that the Bank of England, like its Federal counterpart, 'keeps one eye on the economy'. If inflation rises, interest rates will usually be increased in order to make credit more expensive and to curb the total supply of money running through the economy. This acts to bring the inflation under control.

The central bank's role

The response to a severe economic downturn is the opposite. Generally central banks will lower interest rates to make credit available to struggling businesses to prevent them from failing, and to increase the amount of money in circulation. The action is designed to boost economic growth at a time when it is otherwise flagging.

Considerable controversy surrounds this activity. Part of the problem is that central banks are in practice closely linked to the political process. They tend to pursue policies that find favour with politicians. Governments dislike economic downturns because the increased unemployment that ensues is often blamed on the government, with a resultant loss of popularity for the governing party.

Central bankers have acted in ways designed to smooth the cycle of economic activity. They have restricted credit and the money supply to restrain the economy when it has been surging ahead at what they regard as an unsustainable pace. Conversely, they have loosened the purse strings with lower interest rates and easy credit when the economy has been contracting.

Some economic analysts take the view that this activity is ultimately unsustainable. They argue that the central banks are misleading businesses with false signals about the real state of the economy, making the demand for, and the supply of, money seem higher or lower than it actually is.

Acting on the signals that credit is cheap, businesses will expand to take advantage of anticipated extra demand. When it fails to materialise, or contracts as the bank's stimulus ceases, business finds itself producing too much and has to cut back. In other words, the effect of the bank was to conceal the downturn for a time, making it into a bigger one when the reality of it finally emerges.

COMPETITION, MONOPOLIES, AND SETTING THE RULES

Competition has enjoyed a good press from those who have written about business, and from those who have succeeded in it:

"Competition is the keen cutting edge of business, always shaving away at costs."

– Henry Ford

"Competition is not only the basis of protection to the consumer, but is the incentive to progress."

– Herbert Hoover

"The price which society pays for the law of competition, like the price it pays for cheap comforts and luxuries, is great; but the advantages of this law are also greater still than its cost – for it is to this law that we owe our wonderful material development, which brings improved conditions in its train. But, whether the law be benign or not, we must say of it: It is here; we cannot evade it; no substitutes for it have been found."

– Andrew Carnegie

"The general fact is that the most effective way of utilizing human energy is through an organized rivalry, which by specialization and social control is, at the same time, organized co-operation."

– Charles Horton Cooley

WHEN AN ECONOMIC EXCHANGE takes place, and each party secures something they value more, and parts with something they value less, they agree a price between them. That price depends in part on the availability of the goods being traded. Something in short supply tends to go for a higher price, and for a lower price when there is a glut of supply.

What makes that happen is competition. For most items that are traded there are other people who want to buy them, and for most items being sold there are other suppliers wanting to sell. In effect people are bidding against one another. The merchant with goods has to recognise that people might choose to buy from another merchant, and the customer with money faces the fact that other people with money might also wish to buy those goods.

The stallholder first offered a small bag of rice for the six fish, and then agreed to a larger bag when the fisherman demurred. He did not do so because he was generous or fair-minded, even though he may well have been both. He did it because the fisherman could otherwise have taken his fish to trade elsewhere, and might never have returned to do business with him again.

Competition works through choice. Those who sell goods can sell them to other buyers, and those who buy them can do so from other suppliers. Both seller and buyer want to do business, because that way they trade up in value and gain wealth. They want to do deals, but have to offer terms sufficiently attractive to stop their potential trading partners dealing with other people instead.

Each tries to entice customers to deal with them instead of with other suppliers, and has to give them a reason to do so. That inducement might be based on location. It could be that the site the merchants have chosen from which to offer their wares is a convenient one. Perhaps it is in a central location that people visit for other reasons, and find it suits them to visit the merchant as they do other things in the area. The stall selling ice cream in the park on a hot summer's day is in a very competitive location because people can patronise it without having to abandon the pleasures of the park to do so.

The merchants' attraction might be based on the quality of their goods, rather than location. The merchant might have chosen to offer goods made more carefully from higher quality materials, and attract customers who value really attractive and well-made goods, even though they might command a higher price. Most products and services on offer cover a range of qualities from cheap and cheerful ones which might not last long to top-of-the-range products that people think are worth paying extra for.

The quality difference might lie in the quality of the workmanship or of the ingredients, or simply in terms of design. For most products there are people who will seek out well-designed goods that look good in addition to serving their function.

Competing on price

The most common form of competition, however, is on price. Merchants compete with one another to offer the keenest price they can for a given level of quality. At the bottom line the merchants have to cover their costs and earn money on their investment. Unless they have some advantage in terms of location or quality, though, they have to charge a price that will persuade potential customers to shop with them instead of turning to one of their rivals.

All other things being equal (which they are often not), a buyer will prefer to pay as little as possible for an identical product because this leaves cash left over to buy other things as well. With the aim of bettering one's condition, having the same amount of goods with more cash left over does more to boost someone's wealth.

The fact that customers seek the lowest price makes suppliers compete. Each would rather do the deals and become richer than see a rival do the same. Each lowers prices to the point where profits are still made, but rivals are undercut. The effect of competition is thus to keep prices down to levels where suppliers make sufficient profit to justify the activity, but not much more. If they try to charge more, they open an opportunity for someone to win the trade by charging less.

If there were no competition, there would be no such downward pressure on prices. There is not, and never can be, 'perfect competition'. In the rough and tumble of the real world, suppliers look at what their rivals are doing and adjust their behaviour accordingly. Sometimes they know what competitors are doing, and sometimes not. Sometimes they respond rapidly, sometimes slowly. They do the best they can with the limited amount of information they have.

It is quite common to have a competitor enter into lines of business that seem prosperous. If someone is making good money by providing a particular product or service, there is a good chance that someone else will want to do likewise. The potential competitor might eye up the business and see how they might perhaps do it more efficiently, and be able to charge prices that will undercut their rivals.

Monopoly

In cases where there is no competition, the supplier has a monopoly, and monopoly suppliers do not feel the same downward pressure on prices. If there are no other suppliers that their customers can turn to, there is less pressure to keep their efficiency high and their prices low. Everybody likes competition when they are buying; no one likes it when they are selling. It is something producers have to put up with.

Even with monopoly sellers there are some restraints on price. Customers might choose alternative or substitute products instead, or choose to go without the product altogether. If someone has a monopoly in a particular market of the supply of bamboo fishing rods, for example, and their prices are thought too high, buyers have the option of choosing fishing rods of reinforced plastic or fibre-glass, or of deciding to take up golf instead. What normally happens in such circumstances is that a rival supplier will step in to offer bamboo rods that undercut the original supplier, thereby ending the monopoly.

In different countries and cultures throughout history, rulers have granted monopolies to favoured subjects, usually after money changes hands, using the state's power to forbid potential competitors from setting up in opposition.

Corrupt suppliers have always been prepared to pay generously for this privilege, knowing that they could charge higher prices and enrich themselves as a result. Equally corrupt rulers have always welcomed the cash that such monopolies brought into their coffers.

King Charles I was reluctant to call another Parliament to vote him money because of its opposition to his rule, and monopolies were one of the devices to which he resorted to find funds elsewhere. In return for large sums of money he granted individual merchants the sole right to sell items like bricks, salt and soap. It added greatly to his unpopularity because the privileged merchants were able to charge high prices to their helpless customers.

Other, less obvious, methods have been used to prevent would-be competitors from entering the market. The state might limit a trade so that only qualified or licensed practitioners can ply it. People who want to set themselves up as hairdressers, for example, might be deterred if the law required them to have two years of training and an appropriate licence to practice their trade. If this were to happen, the price of haircuts would almost certainly rise because of the limits it would place on competition.

It is by no means uncommon for established suppliers to seek laws that will restrict new entrants into their market. By keeping competition down, they keep down the pressure that more of it would bring to bear on their prices. The seats of government in many countries are home to lobby groups that act in the interests of particular trades or professions, rather than those of their customers.

Large firms often welcome complex regulation of their industry because it keeps high the costs of entering their business, and acts as a barrier to potential new suppliers who might want to set up in the same line. One consequence is that prices are higher in the absence of competition than they would be if it were comparatively easy for new firms to start up.

In general, competition will act to break up monopolies if it is allowed to. Some monopolies survive because they control some important part of the production process. A firm might have sole access to a resource needed in manufacture, or it might be in sole possession of the technology required. Even in these cases there is a risk that some substitute might be developed, or that an even newer technology will appear to undermine its monopoly position.

Where there are monopolies, the state often acts to regulate them. In fact competition is the best regulator, and the one most likely to make firms behave in responsible ways and offer value to their customers. Where competition for some reason cannot operate, the state often steps in with rules to make the monopolist do some of the things that competition would have made it do otherwise. In some cases this includes only being allowed to charge prices that are approved by the government. In others it can include a raft of measures to control the quality of service that competition would otherwise promote.

'Natural' monopolies

Some monopolies are called 'natural' monopolies because it is believed that the particular industry lends itself to provision by a monopoly supplier. The provision of water to households is often cited. The cost of having competitors provide separate pipes to each household customer would be prohibitive.

In fact when the UK privatised most of its state utilities in the 1980s, most of the so-called 'natural monopolies' were opened up to competition in the private sector. These included gas, electricity and telephones. It did not need separate pipelines to each house, or cables for electricity. Instead firms compete against one another to supply the gas that goes through the pipeline, or the electricity that goes along the cable.

The state railway monopoly was broken up, and competition was introduced by having different companies bid against one another for the franchise to operate trains on the different routes for a number of years. They bid, in effect, for a time-limited monopoly, and because of the absence of any operating competition once they have won that contract, are tightly regulated by an oversight authority which sets limits on the fares they can charge, and makes requirements about their level of capital investment and the standards of service quality they have to meet.

The telephone service, which had been an all-embracing monopoly when run by the government Post Office, became one of the most competitive in the world after it was privatised. Some developing countries had thought it would need a monopoly to lay the telephone lines that could provide a national service. In the event, the technological innovation of the mobile phone service enabled many of them to bypass that stage altogether, and move straight to a telephone service provided by competing mobile phone companies.

It is in cases where neither innovative reorganisation nor alternative technology can be used to make a service competitive that government makes its strongest case for intervention. Where the UK's former state companies enjoyed some residual monopoly powers, the state regulators set up to oversee their activities placed limits on their prices and set minimum standards of service. Most of them were required to reduce their prices to below those which had prevailed under the full state monopoly.

A market economy is not characterised by large monopoly suppliers, but instead by a constant churn of companies going out of business, being taken over, or of new companies springing into existence. People are looking for opportunities to compete, to spot where they can bring in innovations in technology or working practices to capture a share of the market.

New firms

Firms that fail to keep their output attractive in terms of its quality and price soon find their market share is taken by companies that do. Where they are allowed to operate, and where entry costs are not made too high by regulatory requirements, new firms set up to take on the established ones.

Being new has advantages for a firm as well as drawbacks. While it has to get itself established, and has to meet the costs of setting up before any returns from sales start coming in, it might use newer technology and practices than the established firms operate with. Furthermore, it can draw on the experience which others have gained in the market by observing what has and has not worked.

It is also true that well-established firms run the risk of being complacent, and perhaps of taking their customers for granted. The newcomers enter the market with fresh ideas and enthusiasm, and make more effort to win business. They try harder.

The key to this competitive churn which acts to prevent or break up monopolies is that new firms must be able to enter the market. Very often it is the regulatory regime which acts to prevent this by imposing high costs on any new start-ups. Large established firms can and do have whole departments to cope with the regulatory compliance required by government, but new firms, which usually start small, can find the costs of compliance prohibitive.

Monopolies, left unprotected by government, can often be broken by a competitor using new technology or practices to capture a share of their market. In any generation the seemingly dominant companies are mostly different from those which ruled the market a few decades previously. What started as small competitors grew to become the new giants that took the places of the old.

Competition, rather than monopoly, is the norm, but the actions of legislators, sometimes well-meant, can impede its progress. This means that regulation can sometimes be counter-productive. Intended to protect the consumer in cases of monopoly or near-monopoly, it can sometimes make it more difficult for a newcomer to enter the market and protect the consumer better by its competition.

When the UK state monopoly telephone service was turned over to the private sector, one of the strongest concerns was to introduce competition. It was felt that its benign effects would improve the service better than could a regulatory panel telling the industry how it should behave. A small competitor was admitted at the time of privatisation, and six more were later permitted to enter the market, and then more still. The result was that most of the improvements to telephone services have been driven by innovators seeking to anticipate and meet the needs of the public, instead of by the orders of a government panel.

One of the problems with government panels, and with regulators in general, is that they are often directed by people who have little knowledge of the industry they are charged to regulate. The legislators tend to have political rather than commercial experience, and most administrators have experience of public affairs rather than business. The result can be regulation that is ill-judged, inappropriate, and ultimately damaging to the industry.

When competition directs producers to meet the wishes of their customers, it is usually more responsive and more flexible, and on the whole has a better success rate. So although there is a place for regulation, it is by no means as effective as competition at keeping firms on their toes and responsive to consumer wishes.

One place where regulation itself can be used to promote competition is in the break-up of cartels. When firms agree with one another to fix prices, the group which does so is called a cartel or price-ring, and its aim is to replace competition with agreement, in order to keep prices higher than competition might have made them. Not surprisingly, this is regarded as against the public interest and is illegal in most countries.

Adam Smith warned of the temptations to suppress competition:

"People of the same trade seldom meet together, even for merriment and diversion, but the conversation ends in a conspiracy against the public, or in some contrivance to raise prices."

Critics of competition

Can there ever be too much competition and too many choices? In general, if there is profit to be made by offering goods and services it is because the public want to buy them. The choices and varieties on offer suggest sufficient demand for producers to find it profitable to provide them. Some critics complain about all the different varieties of milk that are sold and ask whether we really need that many. But the fact is that some people want full cream milk, others want semi-skimmed, 2 per cent fat, half a per cent fat, and so on. Still others buy goat's milk or milk from Jersey cows.

Adam Smith's dictum is relevant: "The end of all production is consumption." It is because there are customers out there for all of the many varieties of milk that they are to be found on the shelves. The critics who complain about all the choices obviously do not themselves feel the need for all those varieties, but some people seem to. A call for others to be limited to the choices that satisfy critics is really a call for other people to be denied the choices they make themselves, and restricted to whatever the critics think ought to be sufficient for them.

Some critics of competition have described it as 'wasteful', pointing to the economic effort that goes into some unsuccessful businesses, and into the products that fail to capture a profitable share of the market. Far better, suggest some, to direct that effort into successful production instead.

It is in fact competition which determines success. We do not know in advance what products will sell and which companies will succeed. It is the market which tests these things and gives its prizes to those who successfully anticipate popular tastes and preferences. The public expresses its preferences through its choices, and while we can guess what they might be, we will not know reliably until they are made.

Governments which have tried to abolish or seriously restrict competition in their economies have not done very well. The former Communist economies did not allow companies to produce goods on the basis of anticipated demand, but decided centrally in committees what goods should be produced and in what quantities. There was no competition and no market in which consumers could express preferences and decide winners and losers. The absence of competition led to shoddy goods, chronic shortages and interminable queues for the goods that did reach the shops.

It also led to a dull uniformity of production. It is easier, under central planning, to produce standardised products rather than the enormous variety of styles, sizes and colours which competitive markets find space for. The market has space for many winners. The product that fails to come first in popular preferences might sell if its price is reduced. Some people will settle for lower quality if they can obtain it at lower prices.

Competitive markets are extraordinarily good at permitting many different tastes to be satisfied simultaneously. Not everyone wants the top product at the top price, and not everyone wants the same style or colour. Human beings are as different in their characters and preferences as they are in their values, and competitive markets allow niche producers to cater for large numbers of different tastes. The old Communist economies were put to shame by the dazzling profusion of varieties and colours which filled the shelves of Western stores and supermarkets.

Committees are not very good at calculating what goods should be produced and in what quantities and varieties. The reason is that there is just too much information needed. Since individuals differ from one another, information would really be needed about all of them. This is a task too complex for humans, even armed with super-computers. Yet competitive markets manage it every day, making available for each of us the unique mix of products and services that give expression to our individual tastes and preferences.

TAXES

All over Britain tourists stare in fascination at old houses with some of their windows bricked-up. Where there was clearly once a window, there are now bricks or plaster. Sometimes whole terraces exhibit this strange phenomenon. It dates back to 1696 when King William III, William of Orange, introduced a tax on windows. It was not intended to hit poor people, for cottages were exempt. Other houses, though, had to pay 2 shillings annually (a tenth of a pound) if they had fewer than 10 windows, 6 shillings if they had between 10 and 20, and 10 shillings for those with more than 20 windows.

The response of many people was to escape the tax by bricking up windows, and all over England this was done. New houses were built with fewer windows to avoid the tax. When it was extended to Scotland in the 1780s the same happened there, with some opting for the less costly recourse of painting their windows black, with a surrounding white frame. These were known as Pitt's Pictures, after the prime minister of the day, and can still be seen in places.

The tax was increased many times, especially during the wars with France, but it was halved by the reforming administration of 1823, and ended altogether in 1851.

RULERS HAVE LONG made their subjects pay for the expense of being ruled, for the right to farm the land ceded to them by their ruler, and for any protection that ruler afforded from both foreign invaders and domestic criminals. Taxes were well known in the civilisations of ancient Egypt and Babylon, and have taken many forms throughout history.

Rulers have taxed just about everything at one time or another. Taxes have been imposed on lands, on people, on property, on imports and exports, on travel and on transactions. There have been taxes on both necessities and luxuries.

Cooking oil was taxed in Egypt, windows in England, molasses in the American colonies, and strong drink and tobacco in many countries. Taxes have been levied on newspapers and legal documents, on fuel, and on what people earn, on what they spend, and even on what they save.

Modern states rely heavily on income taxes, sales taxes, value added taxes (e.g. VAT), excise duties, corporation taxes, capital gains taxes and inheritance taxes, to name but a few.

Taxation obviously affects economic activity, making many items more expensive than they would otherwise be. With a straight sales tax this is usually transparent, but other taxes can have an impact upon what things cost. A payroll tax, for example, makes it more expensive to employ the people who work to produce the goods, and thus puts up the price of those goods.

Taxes that fall on anything involved in the production process will be incorporated into its costs and augment them. This applies to the land and buildings used for factories, to the energy used to power the machines, and to the raw materials used in production, especially where these have to be imported. Payroll or 'National Insurance' taxes on those who work in production have to be included. Then it applies to the transport of the finished goods if the vehicles and the fuel used are subject to tax. At the point of sale there might be additional business taxes charged on the shops and stores used to sell them, as well as on the actual sales transactions.

At almost every point in the production of goods and services comes government with its hand extended, adding to the costs throughout, and skimming off some of the proceeds of the activity. The first impact of all this tax falls on prices, but there is also the brake it puts on economic activity in general. Because things cost more, fewer transactions take place, and the wealth-creating process which comes about when people trade up for higher value is slowed down.

Taxes thus inhibit economic growth, and higher taxes inhibit it more. They do it selectively, usually having most impact on the areas they fall hardest upon. Rather than pay the higher taxes, some people will opt instead to do more of the things which attract lower taxation. If distilled spirits are taxed more than beer or wine, those who would otherwise drink them might turn to wine or beer instead.

Avoiding taxation

So taxes not only limit the amount of economic activity, they also redirect it. Taxation changes behaviour, a fact increasingly used in modern times to direct people away from activities the government disapproves of, and towards other things instead. The very high taxation of cigarettes is a case in point. Part of its purpose is to discourage the activity. The same is said of alcohol duties.

Most tax-induced behaviour changes are not intentional, however. Government might not be seeking to change the behaviour of its subjects, but simply raising revenue, and then finding that behaviour changes in response to the taxes it imposes. This often happens unexpectedly, causing the tax to yield less revenue than the government thought it would.

This is particularly true when there is a tax boundary which people can choose to stay beneath. The earlier mentioned window tax unintentionally directed people to ensure their houses had fewer windows so they would fall into a lower tax bracket. A householder with ten windows had an incentive to brick up one of them; someone with 24 windows faced a temptation to brick up five of them.

The same effect is seen today in the taxation on house sales. Typically this falls at different rates on more expensive properties, tempting those who buy to look at ones just below such a boundary, and tempting the sellers to settle for a price that is pennies below one.

Taxation adds a new element to each transaction affected by it. After the window tax was introduced, people built houses not with the number of windows they wanted, but with a number that would lighten their tax burden. People who already had a house with their preferred number of windows changed their preference. What had been largely an aesthetic and convenience choice now became much more of a financial one.

There is also a straightforward effect that taxation has on the general economy, in that it reduces disposable income. When people have part of their wages or salaries taken by government, they have fewer resources to spend. The number and value of goods they can afford is diminished. This means a lower level of demand for the goods and services produced by private businesses, and less opportunity for them to make sales and profits. This in turn means that fewer people will be employed in producing those goods and services.

Governments need taxation, however, to pay their way and to engage in the projects that society decides should be done collectively. These include the administration of justice, the police, and the armed forces, and in most societies they include provision for the care of those unable to look after themselves. In many societies government funds collective provision of education through taxation, and in some societies it provides a degree of healthcare.

Governments in sufficiently wealthy economies provide pensions for the elderly, including those who retire from working in government service. In most countries taxation funds infrastructure such as roads and bridges, and local taxes are often used to fund local projects such as sewage schemes and municipal parks and monuments.

Given that taxation can be used to pay for services and projects that people think are worthwhile, the problem for government treasuries is how to raise the necessary revenues without suffering the economic distortions that taxation brings about.

There is no way to avoid all of the distortion it causes, or of the way it limits economic expansion, so the problem comes down to combining two worthwhile but contradictory things, and achieving some of the benefits of each.

The tax rules

Adam Smith set out four canons which he thought taxation should follow. Firstly, the cost of collection must be low relative to the yield. As much as possible of the money taken out by government should actually reach its destination, rather than be wasted on excessive collection costs.

Secondly, he said that the timing of the tax and the amount to be paid must be certain to the payer. He wanted to rule out discretion by tax inspectors, thinking it a likely source of corruption. It should all be open and above board and clearly set out so that people know what their obligations will be.

Thirdly, he stipulated that the means and the timing of payment must be convenient to the payer. Ideally the tax should fall due when the person due to pay it has received some money. Thus a tax on housing should be payable after rent has been collected.

Adam Smith's fourth canon was that taxes should be levied according to ability to pay. In the interests of fairness as well as efficiency, the taxes should be paid by those with the money to do so. Taxation is not supposed to tip people into starvation, so tax claims on the poor should be very much less than those demanded of the rich.

These canons have been widely accepted in principle, even though many of them might be glossed over in practice. Tax scholars criticise existing taxes and newly proposed ones on the basis of whether they conform to Smith's four canons. And since taxation is now vastly more complicated and more demanding than it was in Smith's day, many people have added new canons to Smith's original four.

Few economic commentators would support a proposed tax if it were shown to bring about major economic distortions. Nor would people readily support a tax which would choke off the growth of the new businesses necessary for future prosperity. Maybe there should be a fifth canon, that no tax should damage or limit the economy out of all proportion to any revenue it raises.

The cost of collection is certainly a factor. The fact that it was too costly or time-consuming for rulers in historical times to visit every household led to the practice of 'tax farming', in which a middle-man would pay the ruler an advance sum for a specified area, and then own the right to collect taxes from the people of that area. This proved hugely unpopular, given that tax farmers were notoriously ready to use whatever strong-arm methods it took to recover their investment from the hapless citizens.

The cheapest taxes to collect are ones that someone else is obliged by law to collect for the government. Income tax is widely collected by PAYE, or pay-as-you-earn, which puts a requirement on employers to calculate and deduct the tax due to the government from their employees, and to send it on. They are not paid for doing this, so from a Treasury point of view it costs little. Of course, it costs the employer a great deal in time and trouble, but this is not a cost which falls on government.

Similarly sales taxes are usually collected by shopkeepers being compelled to add them to the sale price, charge their customers, and remit them to government. Since the shops and their sales staff are not paid by government to do this, this too is a low-cost method of collection from the government's point of view.

Smith's second point, that the amount and timing must be clearly known, makes a strong case against retrospective taxation. If the amount of the tax and the time it must be paid are both known in advance for a particular economic activity, citizens can plan their affairs accordingly. To impose taxes after the activity has taken place exposes the citizen to a capricious authority that violates a fundamental principle of law: that the laws must be known in advance.

Taxes should be charged where possible from a stream on income, so the citizen can deduct the portion due to the Treasury. Taxes on income are deducted from wages, and those on sales come from the purchase price as it is handed over. It is easier for a taxpayer to come up with money if it is due at the point when they receive money themselves.

For this reason taxes on wealth are widely unpopular. To be taxed annually on something a person owns, rather than on any income derived from it, is thought to violate tax fairness. It is, in effect, confiscation by instalments. The least popular taxes are ones which require people to eat into their existing wealth to pay them, instead of being taken as a percentage of some increase in wealth.

Fairness

The fourth point Smith makes is one generally accepted as fair. We do not expect richer people to pay more for their milk or their biscuits, but most people think it fair that they should pay more for the services and the protection they receive from the state. Insofar as they have more property, they have more to protect. An equally strong argument is that they can better afford it. Taxes on a poor person might severely constrain their lifestyle, reducing the money they have for life's essentials. To a rich person the tax is more likely to cut into their command of luxury items, so it is widely accepted that most taxes should be paid by people who can afford them.

The term 'regressive' is used for a tax that hits poor people harder. A tax on food, for example, would hit poor families because they spend a higher share of their income on food. A 'progressive' tax on the other hand is one that sees the rich paying a greater share of it. William III's window tax was designed to be progressive by exempting the cottages in which the poor dwelt, and by increasing the tax according to the number of windows. The reasoning was that rich people lived in bigger houses, and these usually had more windows.

Whatever rate is set for income tax sees rich people paying more because they earn more. But income tax is usually made more progressive by levying higher rates on higher earnings. Poor people might be asked to pay 20 per cent, for example, but income above a certain level might incur a 40 per cent rate. Another way of making income tax progressive is to have it start only at a level above the incomes of the lowest earners. This sees the high earners paying income tax, and the poor paying none at all. Both methods are in accord with Smith's fourth canon.

Sales taxes tend to be regressive, in that poorer people spend a higher proportion of their income, but they can be made somewhat progressive by having different rates for different types of item. Low earners do not tend to buy many luxury yachts, for example, so a higher sales tax on these and similar items can make sales taxes more progressive than they would otherwise be.

Changing behaviour

When people make decisions in their "constant, and uninterrupted" effort to improve their condition, they do so in the light of what information they have about the various options available to them. Taxation changes those options, and therefore changes their behaviour. It makes some courses of action less attractive than they would have been without the taxation, and some more attractive.

People might buy cigarettes in one place, for example, because the extra travel time and costs of going somewhere else make it not worth their while. However, an increase in the tax on cigarettes in the place they used to buy them from might justify the extra travel costs in their eyes. The tax authorities who raised the cigarette tax probably assumed that existing customers would pay it, and bring them extra revenue. Now they have altered the differential, however, they find people crossing borders to buy their cigarettes in lower tax areas, making a nonsense of the anticipated revenue increases.

This happens in practice with cigarette taxes whenever people have a practical alternative option. In the US they cross state lines; in the EU they cross national borders. The proportion of cigarettes on which no domestic tax has been paid rises dramatically with each tax increase.

Behaviour changes in another way, too, one probably more favoured by governments. Sometimes when taxes are increased on items, people stop consuming them. Higher cigarette taxes can lead to more people giving up, or at least cutting down, on smoking them. The authorities might favour this for health reasons, but it reduces the revenue they anticipated from the increase.

Income taxes have a different effect. When they are increased, it means that the rewards which come from work are less attractive. People have less money to take home if the government is taking it instead. If work is less rewarding, it means that leisure becomes relatively more attractive, leading some people to choose more of it and do less work.

Instead of putting in extra effort to earn more money, they find the rewards now insufficient, and do other things instead. The tax collectors who thought the higher taxes would bring them more money can now find it brings them less. They are taking a higher percentage, but on a reduced amount of work and wages.

Another unintended consequence can also thwart the government's intentions. People might grumble about taxes, as they always do, but pay them if they are low enough. When they are raised, people might take steps to avoid paying them. A legal way is for earners to use the tax rules to seek out exemptions that shelter their income. They might use off-shore investments, or trust funds, or whatever attracts lower tax rates. This is tax avoidance and is perfectly legal.

Those less concerned with the niceties of the law are tempted to conceal their incomes by dealing in cash or not declaring their full incomes or paying their full liabilities. This is tax evasion, and is a criminal offence.

Either way, the tax authorities who calculated what the increased rate would bring in find themselves thwarted by the behaviour changes it has provoked, and make less than they had supposed.

In some cases tax decreases actually produce higher revenues. In both the UK and the US there were substantial reductions in income tax rates in the 1980s, and in both countries revenues from those taxes were increased. The rates might have been lower, but the total amount of economic activity was higher, so the tax yield increased.

The other curious feature of those tax rate reductions was that better-off people ended up paying a higher share of the total take of income tax than they had when rates were significantly higher. The rate might have been lower, but the extra business, work, and economic activity it encouraged among top earners saw their contribution rise. The top ten per cent of earners in Britain went from paying just over a third of total income tax to paying just under half.

Business taxes

Tax authorities have to tread a fine line when they levy taxes on business. They want a share of the wealth that economic activity is generating, but they want to avoid driving it away, and today it is increasingly mobile.

When rulers taxed land, it could not move away. Even after the industrial revolution when they taxed manufacturing industries, the factories could only be moved at great cost and with great difficulty. In modern times it is easier. In a global economy manufacturers can flee over-burdensome taxes by shutting down production in one country, and transferring it to somewhere with a friendlier (meaning lower) tax policy. It is a costly exercise, but high taxes can make it worth doing.

For the financial services which form an increasing feature in many modern economies, movement is easy. Much of their work is done using modern communication that can be done from almost anywhere. Large banks, investment funds and insurance companies can shut down their operations and re-open them elsewhere with barely a flutter in their activities.

Some governments have adjusted their behaviour accordingly by making themselves attractive to business by implementing low tax rates. In the European Union the Republic of Ireland enticed many businesses to locate within its borders by dramatic reductions in its corporation taxes, taking the rate down progressively from 32 per cent to 12.5 per cent. Revenues soared as a result, and some of the new EU members in Eastern Europe copied Ireland's example and saw similar results.

The basic lesson for tax authorities is that modern technology has combined with globalisation to make business much more mobile than before. Taxation changes behaviour, and one of the behaviour options now available is for business to move to another tax jurisdiction. There is, in effect, competition between tax authorities to make their own location more attractive to businesses. Whereas previously each tax authority might have been tempted to levy higher taxes on business, they now find they must have tax rates sufficiently benign to prevent firms from exercising their option to move away.

Business is mobile, and investment money is mobile. Funds which control billions, even trillions, of dollars can decide where to base themselves based on the taxation, and to some extent the regulation, which prevails in each location. Land cannot move; factory production is difficult to move; financial services can move with relative ease; and capital can move at the touch of a button. Within seconds hundreds of billions can move out of one country and into another.

National treasuries have had to adjust their ambitions accordingly. Taxes on business have been popular with politicians because they fall on individual citizens only indirectly, and few voters attribute the increased costs of products and services to the legislators who brought them about. They have been for governments the goose that laid the golden egg, but in the modern world that goose takes to the air more easily than it did, and it can choose to lay its eggs elsewhere.

What governments have to be especially careful about are taxes on capital. Capital provides the investment for the next generation of businesses, as well as for the increased productivity and expansion of existing ones. It creates the wealth of an economy's future, and is ultimately the source of future employment. Without capital there is no production, and without production there is no employment, no goods to trade, and no new wealth created.

Of all the things which governments tax in their search for revenues to finance their spending, capital is probably the most mobile. It can move in a flash, and seeks out places that will bring high but reasonably secure returns. When governments tax it, they reduce those returns and make other places more attractive by comparison.

From a tax point of view it is in a country's long-term interest to have a large pool of capital invested in its businesses and available to finance new businesses. This arrangement secures a steady flow of jobs, and means that as some businesses become outdated, there are resources available to finance new ones to take their place. It means a steady flow of profits that can be taxed, and employee salaries that can be taxed.

Unfortunately, few governments think in the long term. In democratic countries, politicians' focus tends to be on the next election, and there is a standing temptation to implement policies which will bring immediate gain, even if the longer-term consequences are adverse. Higher taxes imposed upon capital now might bring in money to finance popular projects that will win legislators re-election, but only at future cost to an economy as capital drains away to more amenable places. Politicians tend to think that the future will be someone else's problem.

In recent times advancing technology and ease of transport has meant that individuals are also more mobile. They can cross borders and choose to settle in tax-friendly places. It is particularly true of talented individuals at the top end of the financial and knowledge industries. To an increasing extent many of them can choose where they wish to live and work, and tax rates feature among the factors influencing their choices.

There are other factors, such as a low crime rate, the cost of living, the presence of good schools, transport infrastructure, and even good leisure facilities such as restaurants, theatres and golf courses. But tax rates play their part, and governments have to watch that high rates of personal taxation do not drive talented high earners to take their abilities and their earnings elsewhere.

The fifth canon

That fifth canon that might be added to Adam Smith's four, the one saying that no tax should damage or limit the economy out of all proportion to any revenue it raises, would certainly limit taxes that might be imposed. If the revenue a tax raises would be insignificant compared to the damage and distortion it inflicts, it shouldn't be imposed in the first place.

In practice there is a problem with most taxes: the future is uncertain. Since taxation changes behaviour, no one can know in advance how much money any individual tax will raise. Calculations and estimates can be made, but time after time they fail to predict accurately how much each tax will bring in. The reason is that the calculations are usually based on how people behave with taxation at its current level, and fail to predict how behaviour will alter when it is changed.

Nor can anyone be sure how much economic damage or distortion will be wrought by any particular tax. Again, it might be estimated, but the reality of what happens is only evident when we look back at it, and even then experts disagree about which causes led to which events. There is always so much going on in an economy that it is difficult to isolate the effect of any individual item.

We might be confident that an announced increase in a tax will lead to people rushing to complete transactions before it takes effect, or that an announced reduction will lead them to postpone transactions until the lower rates prevail. But we never know in advance how much of this will happen, or to what degree the changes will lead people to substitute some economic decisions for others.

This uncertainty makes that fifth canon difficult to apply in practice. The Treasury might propose a tax and put a figure on the revenue they expect from it, but analysts might examine the history of similar taxes and conclude that it will cause more damage than it is worth. This is one reason why tax policy is so controversial; no one can know until afterwards.

Difficult though these calculations are, governments and their treasuries owe it to their citizens to make the attempt. Any proposed tax change should be thought through, looking at the possible and likely behaviour changes it might instigate, and trying to predict the sort of effects they might have on the wider economy, as well as on the yield which the individual change might bring. The odds are high that if this were to be done, many of the tax changes that subsequently fall at the first hurdle would never leave the starting gate.

INTERNATIONAL TRADE

Jake spends a long time choosing a pair of jeans. This time he decides on stone-washed blue ones with orange stitching. He has found in the past which brands give him a better fit, but fashion sits high on his list of priorities. It's important to choose a fashionable brand, as well as one that looks good on him.

The jeans he eventually buys are, like most jeans, made of cotton twill with the distinctive weave that characterises denim. Several complex processes have been gone through in different places to put together the finished product.

The cotton might have been grown in many countries, including India, Turkey and the United States, and had to be turned first into thread, and then into fabric. The indigo used to dye them originally came from tropical plants, but these days is usually made synthetically, perhaps in Germany.

Stone-washing makes the cloth softer, and is done by washing the cloth in a rotating tub with light stones alongside. These might be pumice, mined in the Italian volcanic island of Lipari, amongst other places. The copper from which the orange rivets are made probably comes from Chile, and had to be mined, smelted and shaped. Zinc, perhaps mined in Canada, had to be alloyed with copper to make brass that could be shaped into segments for the zip fastener.

The leather patch that declares the maker's name above the back pocket could have come from Argentina or North Africa, and had to be cured and tanned. The jeans Jake chose were sewn on machines in China, but he could have picked ones made in Thailand, the Philippines, or in a variety of Asian countries.

In all of the places where the constituent parts of his garment were processed, there could be teenagers like himself working full-time or part-time to earn income for themselves and their families. People from many countries played a role in producing his jeans, but it is highly unlikely that Jake will ever meet any of them, or that they will ever meet one another. Nonetheless, they all played a part in the process, and co-operated unwittingly in producing the finished garment.

THE DRIVING FORCE behind much international trade is specialisation. Many products are made up of different components, some of which come from different countries. International trade makes international specialisation possible, with production lines using components imported from many countries.

The same process takes place when people of different countries trade as occurs when people of the same town or village trade with one another. In each transaction the participants exchange what they already have for what they would rather have, be it money or goods.

Jake wanted the jeans more than the money he exchanged for them, and the same was true of the people who picked the cotton, wove the cloth, made the dye, mined the pumice, the copper and the zinc, cured the leather, and sewed the jeans. In each case they valued the money they received higher than the labour they put in or the time they spent doing it.

None of them particularly intended to do favours for other people. They might well all have been considerate and generous people, but that is not why they made their contribution. They did that to improve their own condition, and by doing so co-operated unwittingly with one another.

Many other people were involved as well. There were the people who worked for the company that made and marketed the jeans, the advertising agency which promoted the brand, the employees of the distributors and of the retail outlets that sold them. If all of the people who had helped to produce Jake's jeans and make them available for him to buy were lined up and counted, there would be dozens of them, perhaps hundreds. And they would come from many different cultures and countries.

Just as specialisation increased productivity when practised within a pin factory or a family shoe-making business, so it does within countries on the international scale. One worker can specialise in what he or she can do best and most efficiently, and so can a country concentrate its capital and resources on what it does best.

Self-sufficiency

It is a common error to suppose that it is good for a country to be self-sufficient, and to not depend on imports for some of its goods and services. This mistake is as erroneous as the one that tells us that countries get rich by exporting, and then hoarding the precious metals they receive in return.

Few of us would call a family sensible if the family members made their own shoes, baked all their own bread, made their own bicycles, and so on. Other people do these things better and cheaper by specialising, and the sensible family buys them in and becomes richer by having wealth left over to spend on other things.

It is similar with countries. They could all try to be self-sufficient at great expense, but it makes more sense to import particular goods from countries that have specialised in making them more efficiently, either in price or quality. Adam Smith gave a famous example about how wines could be made in Scotland:

"By means of glasses, hotbeds, and hot walls, very good grapes can be raised in Scotland, and very good wine too can be made of them at about thirty times the expense for which at least equally good can be brought from foreign countries."

It would, he said, be a manifest absurdity to ban the import of foreign wines into Scotland so that its own could be sold there instead. By buying foreign wines at one thirtieth of the cost, the Scots were left with twenty-nine thirtieths to spend on other things. In other words, they were richer.

Anyone who has lived in Scotland might doubt whether the Scots climate would ever permit "very good wine" to be made there, but even if it could, it would only be at greater cost, and almost certainly would be less good than that which could be imported more cheaply. The French, meanwhile, might try to produce malt whisky, but lacking Scotland's natural advantages of the appropriate peat, distinctive water and barley, and centuries of loving expertise, it is doubtful they could produce anything approaching the quality of the Scottish product, even at many times the cost.

The lesson is clear, and people have learned it. French wine sells in Scotland, and Scots malt whisky in France, with both countries getting a better deal than if they had tried to make both products themselves. Countries sell what they are good at, be it by a natural advantage of climate, geography or geology, or even a long tradition of expertise. They buy from other countries what similarly enjoys an advantage there, and everyone benefits.

Protectionism

Misguided governments, often motivated by the mercantilist fallacy (the view that countries become wealthy by exporting as much as possible while importing as little as they can), have sought to promote domestic competitors to foreign imports in a policy called 'protectionism'. The usual tools are subsidies and tariffs. Subsidies give domestic producers money from taxpayers so they can sell their products more cheaply, even though they are more costly to produce. And tariffs put taxes on imported goods to make them more expensive to buy than locally produced ones. Both of them make populations poorer than they would have been without them.

It is, however, popular politically for legislators to be seen to be protecting domestic jobs, and electors vote for it without realising that it is done at their expense. If local jobs are protected by subsidies, it means that taxpayers are paying more money to the government so that domestic producers can charge them what foreigners would have charged them without the extra taxes. They are therefore poorer. If local jobs are protected by tariffs, it means that consumers have to pay more for foreign products to stop them being cheaper than domestic ones. Once again, they are poorer.

The claim is often made that the foreign competition is 'unfair'. They might pay their workers lower wages because they are still a developing economy and are trading on that advantage. Perhaps they have access to cheaper raw materials, and are exploiting a natural advantage. Maybe their industries are not burdened with mountains of regulations and they are able to produce more efficiently in consequence. What 'unfair' usually comes down to meaning is 'cheaper'.

The French writer Frédéric Bastiat produced a humorous spoof letter allegedly from French candle-makers, complaining about an 'unfair' competitor, namely the Sun. Because it produced its light without cost, it was undercutting the candle-makers, and they therefore demanded that their government shut out its light by means of mandatory window shades!

Economies are dynamic. They change and develop, and participants have to adapt to changing circumstances. There was a time when Britain was the source of cheap textiles because of the technological advances of its industrial revolution. As other countries have developed, however, they have been able to compete on cheap textiles and undercut British prices. The result has been that many of the Lancashire textile mills have had to close, and their workers have been forced to find other employment.

Neither manufacturers nor their workers like this. Both groups would prefer to continue making a comfortable living in the old ways. To respond to cheaper foreign imports with subsidies and tariffs (and both have been used at various times) is to make domestic consumers pay more than they need for their textiles, and to deny emerging foreign countries the chance to improve the living standards of their citizens.

An alternate response, which some UK textile producers took, is to seek different markets in which they do not face the same degree of competition.

Some manufacturers went up-market towards the quality end of the textile trade, producing more luxurious items and designer-label goods to a market sector prepared to pay higher prices, and they prospered accordingly.

So politically tempting for countries is the alternate route, that of subsidies and tariffs, that there has often been a beggar-my-neighbour approach, with each country trying to subsidise its own production more than its rivals, and each imposing tariffs on what others produce. The result has been mutual impoverishment, with the citizens of each country as the losers, paying more in taxes to fund the subsidies, and higher prices for their goods because of the tariffs.

It is to prevent this that countries sometimes agree with one another not to do it. If nobody does it, countries are in the same position as if everybody does it, but without the impoverishing effects. This is what Free Trade is all about, and the World Trade Organization (WTO) is the international body that tries to secure this as widely as possible. Countries must respect its rules to become members, and accept its adjudication. The rewards to its members of being able to trade without hindrance are so great that most countries have signed up to it.

Comparative advantage

Each country prospers by exporting what it does better, and importing what others do better. This is the formula that makes each trading partner wealthier. But suppose, some people say, that one country is more efficient at everything? Perhaps, in addition to the ones it has specialised in and is really good at, it is also better than a trading partner at everything else. Then the other country, probably a poorer one if it is less efficient at everything, will have nothing it can sell.

The 19th century economist David Ricardo showed that this is not true. Even in such cases, he argued, it pays the first country to import whatever the second one does best, even if it can itself do it better. The reason is that by doing so, the first country can specialise still further, and devote even more of its capital and effort to the goods it produces *even* better, and thus have more of its output at a higher margin. It will be concentrating on that which makes it very rich, and letting the other country produce that which would have merely made it somewhat rich.

It works to the advantage of both, and Ricardo's reasoning is called the Theory of Comparative Advantage. It reinforces what we already know about international trade – that it makes both sides richer, be they importers or exporters.

Trade imbalances

What happens when a country finds it cannot sell enough exports to pay for the imports it needs? In this case it has a negative trade balance. Either it can put in extra efforts to export more, or try to import less. In the days before the WTO, which oversees global rules of trade between countries, nations in such circumstances would be tempted to subsidise exports and put tariffs on imports. Because other countries would retaliate, reducing trade and its wealth-creating potential all round, this is now disallowed under WTO rules.

Fortunately there is a much easier solution. Unless the nation's currency is fixed in terms of other currencies, it can 'float' up or down against the others. A country with a negative trade balance will usually find its currency going down somewhat against the others. This has two helpful effects. Firstly, it means that imports become more expensive to its citizens. A pound which is worth one euro will only buy two-thirds as much as one worth 1.5 euros. With imported goods costing 50% more, people buy fewer of them.

It works for exports, too, because a 'weaker', less valuable currency will mean that exports become cheaper to others when its value declines. That British tractor priced at £10,000 used to cost people in the eurozone €15,000, whereas it now costs them €10,000. Other things being equal, a lower price will attract more buyers.

With imports now dearer and exports now cheaper, that negative trade balance is soon corrected. It works the other way around, too, in that countries which export much more than they import find their currencies floating up in value on the money markets, so their exports become dearer and their imports cheaper. Again, the currencies adjust to correct the imbalance.

If a country has fixed exchange rates, set in terms of another currency such as the US dollar, they can still correct negative trade imbalances, but in such cases it has to be by devaluing their currency, setting it at a lower rate against others. While this also works, it is more abrupt and more painful than the steady readjustments which take place all the time with floating currencies. It causes political problems, too, since devaluation is seen as a humiliating pointer to a country's weaker economic status, and tends to diminish the respect accorded to the politicians who undertake it.

GLOBALISATION AND DEVELOPMENT

Caroline was really looking forward to the picnic, but she had responsibilities. She and Dan were in charge of the food, which seemed only fair if Cynthia and Sam were organising the drinks. The easiest, thought Caroline, would be salmon and cucumber sandwiches on wholemeal bread with mayonnaise, lemon and black pepper inside. But what should follow? The dessert needed to be easily carried and not something that would disintegrate in transit.

Then she had the perfect idea: a mixed fruit salad. She strolled over to the supermarket's fruit counter and made a quick selection. She began with the berries, and chose blueberries, blackberries and strawberries, all Spanish. Those Australian plums looked good, so she picked out a few. Then she added apples from New Zealand, pears from the Netherlands, fresh white grapes from India, and seedless red ones from Chile. She selected clementines from Argentina. Greek nectarines and Italian peaches were next, and then she decided to add a tropical touch with a mango from Mali, passion fruit from Colombia and a huge Costa Rican pineapple.

Some of the fruit would need to be peeled, some stoned, and some simply washed, but Caroline went home pleased with her choices. They'd go very well together. She'd remembered just in time to add paper dishes and plastic spoons to her shopping. This was going to be a picnic to remember, and she hoped Cynthia and Sam would make as good a job with the drinks.

PEOPLE HAVE ALWAYS traded beyond their territorial borders. Archaeologists tell us that the remains of ancient settlements often contain non-native products. Things like obsidian and amber are found hundreds, even thousands, of miles from their source, and analysis of metal artefacts reveals their use far from the places where their ore was mined and smelted.

Ships filled with cargoes were sailing the seas thousands of years ago, and beasts of burden laden with goods have trodden trade trails for probably longer. What is new about modern globalisation is the scale of it and the depth of international trade. Modern communication and transport have made widespread trade possible, but it has also happened because people wanted it to. International agreements have been reached to facilitate and promote trade because its value has been recognised.

Most, if not all, of the world's countries now trade with one another to some degree, and technological improvements have certainly made this easier. Extensive railways, heavier trucks, container ships and jumbo jets all play their part in shifting goods more easily, and in relative terms more cheaply, than was previously possible.

It used to be the case that expensive goods were transported to faraway places because the transport costs were only a small fraction of their worth. The same applied to light manufactured goods, but developments in transport have now made possible the transport and distant sale of very low cost items. Thanks to the cargo holds of jumbo jets, even perishable items can now be sent for sale overseas, including the fruits that Caroline chose for her fruit salad in the above story.

There used to be seasons for eating fruit in Britain. Strawberries were a treat of early summer, then plums in the summer, and then apples would come in the early autumn, followed by blackberries. British fruit still has its seasons, but now thanks to globalisation, families can eat almost any fruit the whole year round. People still make English summer pudding, but now the blueberries, raspberries and strawberries that go into it are available all year round.

Some say this is not a good thing, on the grounds that global transport has smoothed out regional variations in foods, and ended the eager anticipation with which people used to await the first strawberries of the year, or the season's first asparagus. Others counter this by pointing to the extra choices families now have.

More seriously, some environmentalists deplore the fuel used to ship these foods around the world when we should, they say, be content with what is grown locally. They talk of the 'food miles' involved in the foods we import.

There seems to be a version of the mercantilist fallacy just below the surface of this claim. It is a call for choices to be restricted, and for people to be obliged to buy more expensive local items instead of cheap foreign ones, whereas the norm has been that the wider we trade, the greater the prosperity achieved. Distant trading allows for more competition, with its downward pressure on prices.

As for 'food miles', many of the locally grown competitors are far more energy-intensive than their imported rivals. Tomatoes grown in Italy under free sunshine are more environmentally friendly than ones grown in the UK in heated greenhouses, even when the transport fuels are factored in. Often it is sunshine that is being imported as well as foodstuffs. The Mediterranean or tropical sun might offer unfair competition to UK farmers, just as it did to French candle-makers, but the sensible course would be to produce something else instead, items that can be done better and cheaper in Britain.

Manufactured goods

Globalisation has had a no less dramatic impact on manufactured goods, especially of household items and clothes. In Britain people used to buy large numbers of goods like these manufactured in Britain itself or in other European countries. Now our marketplace is practically the entire world. We buy white goods like refrigerators and washing machines, plus electronic items and even cars from the Far East, from where a variety of different countries supply them.

In many cases these goods cost much less than their equivalents could be made for in Europe. It has been a benign exchange on the whole. We buy them and the money we save makes us richer. They sell them and the money they earn makes them richer.

The drawback is that the workers in Europe who used to make these goods now have to turn their hand to other things. Globalisation has in effect brought over a billion low-wage workers in developing countries onto the world marketplace. Their unskilled labour now competes with unskilled labour in developing countries, undercutting its costs. The result has been a decline in the proportion of low-skill manufacturing jobs in richer countries.

Many more people in Britain are now employed in service industries instead of in manufacturing. Even in manufacturing, where the UK used to compete on price, it now has to do so on quality. Britain now makes high quality steels, since it cannot compete with the cheap steels coming from the Far East. It specialises in heavy engineering, the machines that run factories or help to build infrastructure, since it cannot match the Far East in electric toasters and televisions.

When faced with international competition they cannot match, and faced with losing their industries, countries have the choice of moving up-market into areas where they can compete on quality and design, or of moving to new industries altogether.

International outsourcing

Quite a large proportion of the goods imported into advanced countries from developing ones do so at the behest of Western companies, and bear their brand names. Typically the established Western company will outsource the manufacture of its products or of their components to cheaper factories abroad. Goods bearing the brand of familiar household names are produced, often in Asia, and shipped to Western markets to be sold.

This enables established firms to maintain their competitiveness by keeping prices down, but it employs far fewer people in developed countries. There are still jobs in design, marketing, advertising, distribution and sales, but the manufacturing jobs are now overseas.

The computer firm Apple has many of its products actually made in places like Taiwan and China, but all of the other jobs associated with them are located in developed countries. The same is true of many, if not most, of the firms which sell manufactured consumer goods. The actual production is done out East, but the other jobs stay at home.

This type of transfer tends to mean that jobs in the richer countries have moved to being cleaner, less physically demanding, and less dangerous, as well as being better paid than the old jobs were. It is also true that most of the money that people pay for consumer goods does not go out East, but stays in the developed country. The actual manufacturing cost is often a fraction of the total, with the rest going into all of the associated jobs mentioned above, the ones that stay in the West.

Globalisation has brought cheaper goods to Western markets by integrating lower-cost labour in developing countries into the world economy. It has also brought huge benefits to the developing countries, above and beyond the wages paid to their workforce. It has brought in Western capital and technology, and seen outside investment pour in to develop factories and production processes.

The integration of most countries into a world economy has brought about a huge increase in wealth, not only in the rich countries, but with a significant share in the developing countries themselves. The two largest, China and India, have seen increases in living standards unparalleled in their history, with China's growth averaging nearly 10 per cent per annum, and India's near 8 per cent. Other countries, too, have set their feet firmly on the ladder of economic growth.

The last quarter of a century has seen more people lifted out of poverty than has ever happened since human beings first began to walk upright. Globalisation has brought most of the world into a marketplace, able to trade the products of their labour and skills to people in faraway countries. Trade creates wealth, and the most significant impact of globalisation has been the greatest and most rapid wealth-creation that humankind has ever achieved.

Development

There is still a big disparity between living standards in the advanced economies and those in the developing world. On an international scale the gap is narrower than it was because of the rise of some once-poor countries to comparative affluence. After the Second World War there were only a few rich nations, with the rest of the world poor. The rise to affluence of Japan, then of South Korea, Singapore, Hong Kong and Taiwan, has been followed by the economic success of many other countries. Many African countries, however, have enjoyed nothing like the same success and remain with very low per capita incomes.

There are international calls for more aid, for the richer countries to give a higher percentage of their wealth to poorer countries. While aid undoubtedly performs many humanitarian functions such as combating disease and making clean water available, it is not effective in promoting economic development.

Development aid, as opposed to humanitarian aid, has tended to go from government to government, with the rulers of the recipient countries responsible for its allocation. In some countries there have been allegations that much of it has been diverted into corruption, favouring the friends and relatives of the rulers. In others it has been used to back projects favoured by the government, perhaps for political or prestige reasons, rather than for development based on genuine economic demand.

Underlying the economic success stories has not been development aid, but international trade. No country has risen from poverty to comparative affluence because of development aid, and none has done it without trade. The countries which have succeeded developed products they were able to sell. Some have attracted foreign investment to build industries whose goods and services can win a share of world markets.

The money earned by selling goods on international markets can be recycled into further investment and expansion. The rich countries can play a part in this economic development by allowing the goods from poorer countries into their markets so their own citizens can buy them.

While humanitarian aid might be done from the most noble of motives, it is probably more important that rich countries open their markets. People in poorer countries want to sell us their produce. In very many cases it is cheaper, and will sell readily if allowed to compete. Unfortunately the politics of advanced economies often tempts governments into subsidies and tariffs designed to favour their own produce instead.

Of all the policies which have hurt and held back poorer countries, the use of agricultural subsidies by rich countries has been among the most damaging. Developed countries have given huge tax-funded subsidies to their farmers, and put tariffs on many imported foodstuffs. In doing so they have over-encouraged domestic production such that it built up huge surpluses. They have then disposed of these surpluses by selling them on world markets at subsidised prices.

The tariffs stopped poorer countries from selling their foodstuffs to Western countries, and the competition from the subsidised surpluses hindered their chance of selling them on world markets. If a policy were deliberately designed to keep poor countries in poverty, it could hardly do better than those which sustain agricultural subsidies in rich countries.

Most people in advanced economies would like to inhabit a world in which people were not condemned to die of starvation or of preventable diseases. They would like to see people in all countries have access to education and healthcare, together with a decent standard of living. These things take wealth to bring about, not wealth redistributed, but wealth created.

It is trade and exchange that create wealth, and which can, on an international scale, spread their benefits across the globe. Globalisation and international free trade can multiply the opportunities for economic interaction between peoples of all countries, and help them onto the path of wealth-creation.

OVERVIEW

ECONOMIC ACTIVITY IS ABOUT choices, about how time and resources are to be allocated. As individuals we do this in our personal lives, and as citizens we do it collectively through our governments. In both areas we try to do the best we can, knowing that our knowledge is imperfect. No one can ever know all of the facts which might be relevant to an economic decision, and no one can know how the future might turn out. We act with the limited information available to us, and we interact with others who are similarly placed.

We choose to allocate our time and resources in ways that will better our condition, and we try to pick the ways that will do it most effectively. We do so in the knowledge that when we make a choice, it is usually at the expense of the other choices we could have made. We do not have infinite resources or infinite time, so we use our values and preferences to decide between the possible allocations we might make.

The actions we take preclude and forestall the actions we might have taken in their place. When we make a choice we are sometimes not sure if it is the right one, or whether we will have cause to regret not making another one instead. We just do the best we can.

Most of us make a reasonable job of giving expression to our preferences through our choices. Those who say we are simply not equipped or knowledgeable enough to do this sensibly in the modern world can be countered by others who point out that no one is better equipped. We know more about our own life and circumstances and about our tastes and values than others do, and we care more than others do. Furthermore, most of us are competent to watch what other people do, and to seek advice on the more difficult choices.

When people's choices and allocations are expressed collectively through their governments, many of the same principles apply. Governments do not have infinite resources and time, and must make decisions as to which uses should command priority. Each action they take shuts off the other possible actions they might have taken instead. The same cash spent on defence cannot also be spent on education.

Furthermore, most actions by governments preclude the actions that could otherwise have taken place in the private sector of the economy. The reason is that government secures most of its funding from other people. Ultimately it is individuals who contribute to financing government activity. It is taken in taxation, in borrowing which has to be repaid with interest, or by increasing the money supply and reducing the value of everyone else's money.

When government takes money from private citizens, it closes off the economic activity for which they might otherwise have used it. Government might spend money to 'create' new jobs, but in doing so it prevents the economic activity which that same money might have instigated elsewhere. Statistics have shown that money left in private hands might create more jobs than when it is taken and spent by government.

Even taxes on business fall ultimately on individuals, usually in the form of the higher prices they have to pay for what is produced, and sometimes by way of smaller dividends from the company profits once government has taken its cut. All of this is money that could have been spent otherwise.

It is an important point about economics that resources rarely appear out of the blue. Normally they have to be earned by trading, perhaps time and effort for payment, or perhaps some goods for other goods. When those resources are used for one thing, the decision prevents the alternative uses to which they might otherwise have been put.

When government uses its laws and regulations to direct business, more often than not it increases the costs on the businesses it affects, raising the costs and the prices of their goods and services, and making everyone who buys them poorer than they might have been. Tariffs and subsidies might help particular industries to survive foreign competition that might have overwhelmed them, but only at the cost of diminishing the wealth of everyone who buys the goods or who pays the necessary taxes. The monies people have forfeited to sustain tariffs and subsidies would otherwise have sustained other jobs in other companies by purchasing their products.

If there are lessons from this, they should perhaps teach us that few economic actions are as simple as they look. The ripples of unintended consequences spread outward from them, and a hinterland of thwarted possibilities can be wiped from the economic map without even impinging on our awareness.

Economics is indeed intuitive, and it derives from the simple principles which govern our behaviour as we try to improve our condition and interact to mutual advantage with others who are doing the same. From these simple fundamentals a vast and complex economic order is built up, one containing and circulating far more information than any individual or group can hope to apprehend.

The economy behaves with some of the characteristics of an organism, reacting in sometimes delicate and complicated ways to the inputs it receives. Economies, like organisms, are easier to damage than to improve. Some of the actions undertaken by governments with good intentions can inflict untold, and sometimes unseen, damage to the lives of people who are simply doing the best they can to improve their lives, only to find that their circumstances have changed unexpectedly.

Our emerging appreciation of economics has achieved astonishing things. After many millennia of a precarious subsistence, large sections of humankind have managed to achieve a degree of security and comfort that enables them to lead worthwhile and fulfilling lives. Men and women have found how to create wealth by exchange and trade, and how to augment that wealth by investment and entrepreneurship. They have created an expanding economy, and with it all of the possibilities that flow from it.

An understanding of economics has never perhaps been as important as it is now, given the part it plays in all of our lives. The hope must be that those who legislate on our behalf will themselves acquire an understanding and an appreciation of the economy, perhaps learning in the process how to avoid inflicting damage upon it. Then the economies of the world can achieve things that will outshine all that they have done hitherto.

GLOSSARY

Assets

Assets are anything that is owned and has a value that can be measured in money. For a person they might include possessions such as a house, a car or a bank balance. For a company they might include properties, shares, stock, or debts owed to it.

Balance of trade

The balance of trade is the difference in value between what a country sells abroad and that which it buys from other countries. Figures are usually published monthly.

Balance sheet

A balance sheet shows a firm's financial position with regard to its assets and debts.

Basis point

Basis points are used to measure changes in indicators such as interest rates, and a single basis point is equal to one hundredth of one per cent. If an interest rate of 3.00 per cent increases by 10 basis points, it rises to 3.10 per cent.

Basket of currencies

A basket of currencies consists of a chosen group of currencies taken together as a unit. It is a way of protecting against currency fluctuations, because as some currencies in the basket fall in value, others might rise.

Bear market

A bear market is one in which prices are going down. It occurs when investors are pessimistic and sell up now to save them from greater losses in future.

Bond

Bonds are certificates issued by governments and corporations when they borrow money. These bonds are like IOUs that bear annual interest and have to be repaid on a specified date. They can rise or fall in value, depending on what other returns are available elsewhere, and on how confident people are that the issuer will pay the interest and redeem the bond when it falls due.

Boom

An economic boom is said to be happening if the economy is growing and shares are rising in value. It is usually accompanied by a widespread increase in prosperity.

Bubble

A 'bubble' happens when prices of some particular assets rise rapidly without any underlying reason except that buyers think they will rise even more. It is called a bubble if it bursts like a real bubble and prices collapse, although people can only be sure it was a bubble after it has burst.

Bull market

A bull market is one in which prices are rising, and when investors are confident, hoping for more price increases in future. It is the opposite of a bear market.

Capital

Capital is the term used to describe wealth when it is put to work to create more wealth.

Capital gains tax

A capital gains tax is one that is levied on a gain in value of an asset when an investor realises the gain by selling the asset.

Cartel

A cartel is another name for a price-ring. It is an association of producers of similar items who agree amongst each other to keep the price of their goods higher than it would have been if they had competed. A famous example is the Organization of Petroleum Exporting Countries (OPEC).

Cash flow

Cash flow describes the movement of cash into and out of a business as it sells goods or services on the one hand, and pays bills and wages and settles its debts on the other. Cash flow is important because a business needs liquidity to pay its creditors. Inadequate cash flow is a major hazard for new businesses because no matter how profitable they are, they need to have cash coming in to pay their creditors.

Central bank

A central bank is a national or international body tasked by government to issue currency, to provide financial services to governments and commercial banks, and to regulate the activities of private banks. In some countries the central bank is an arm of government, in others it has a degree of independence. Central banks such as the Bank of England set interest rates and are required to control inflation.

Commodities

Commodities are the raw materials of production. They might be agricultural, such as maize or rice, or mineral, such as metal ores and oil.

Consumer Price Index

The Consumer Price Index (CPI) measures the changes over time in the price of a basket of typical goods. It is used as a measure of inflation, and many payments (including wage deals and interest rates offered) can be linked to it. It does not include housing, as the Retail Price Index (RPI) does.

Credit crunch

The credit crunch is the shorthand name given to the financial crisis which started in 2007. Banks were alerted to unknown risks incorporated into their assets that made the value of those assets uncertain. They dramatically reduced their lending to other banks and other would-be borrowers. This resulted in higher interest rates, and made loans hard to secure. Businesses and individuals suffered when credit became harder to obtain.

Default

A default occurs when a debtor fails to meet the obligation to pay the agreed interest on time, or to repay the principal sum lent. A government which fails to pay on time the specified amount on the bonds it issued is said to be in default.

Derivatives

A derivative is a contract that enables someone to trade in an item without actually owning any of it. What they have instead is a security whose price varies with changes in the price of the actual item.

Direct tax

A direct tax is one that is paid directly to the tax authority, such as income tax, VAT, or corporation tax. It contrasts with an indirect tax which is paid by a supplier and passed on in the form of increased prices.

Dow Jones

The Dow Jones Industrial Average, or Dow, is an index of 30 large US companies that indicates how their share prices are performing. It is taken to indicate how the US stock market is performing, much as the FTSE 100 gives the level of UK share prices.

Economic growth

Economic growth represents an increase in a nation's output of goods and services. When it is positive it means that the country is richer.

Elasticity of demand

Demand is said to be elastic when the amount people consume of some goods and services alters when their price changes. It is inelastic if such changes bring about no alteration in demand.

Equity

The equity a person has in a property represents the proportion of it that they own. For a house it is the value minus the remaining mortgage debt. For a company it is the holding they own in it. Sometimes the word 'equities' is used to refer to shares in companies.

Exchange controls

Exchange controls are the controls which a government puts on its citizens to limit the amount of currency that can flow out of or into a country.

Exchange rate

The exchange rate is the rate at which one currency can be exchanged for another. When people travel abroad it tells them how much their own currency is worth in terms of another.

Factory gate prices

Factory gate prices are the prices of goods as they leave the factory, and before the addition of transport costs, wholesale and retail costs, and advertising and distribution costs. It is a useful statistic to know the price of goods 'at the factory gate' because it indicates what they cost to produce.

Fiscal policy

Fiscal policy is the name given to attempts by governments to control economic output by changing their spending levels or by altering tax rates. Typically governments use it in an attempt to increase spending during an economic downturn.

FTSE 100

The FTSE 100, colloquially called the 'footsie', is a share index of the 100 largest UK companies. It is taken as a measure of how the stock market as a whole is performing. The index is compiled by the FTSE Group, a joint venture between the *Financial Times* (FT) and the London Stock Exchange (SE). Whilst its name derives from these parent companies, the acronym stands alone now, registered in its own right.

Futures

A 'future' is a contract under which someone agrees to pay a fixed price for a set quantity of a named asset to be delivered at some agreed date in the future.

Gearing

Gearing (which is sometimes called 'leverage' in the US) refers to the ratio of debt taken on by a company in proportion to its own equity funds. Many companies can make a greater return on borrowed funds than the interest they have to pay on them, so they borrow money to add to their own investment capital.

Globalisation

Globalisation represents trade conducted across national and even intercontinental boundaries. As more countries become part of a single world market, their products, their businesses and their labour are able to buy and sell and to draw on resources in a huge interconnected market operating across most of the planet.

Gross Domestic Product

A country's gross domestic product (its GDP) refers to its production of goods and services. It is a measure of its economic output.

Gross National Product

A country's gross national product (its GNP) is a nation's GDP plus the net inflow of income from abroad.

Hedge fund

A hedge fund is a private investment fund that specialises in complex and unconventional investment strategies to secure higher returns than those available from conventional investments. Intended mainly for experienced investors, hedge funds often attempt to make gains by forecasting changes in asset prices.

Hedging

Hedging involves making investments that protect other investments from future price fluctuations.

Index-linked

Index-linked means tied to the rate of inflation, or inflation-proofed. Index-linked bonds pay interest at a rate that is related to a measure of inflation (such as the CPI). Wages, salaries and pensions that are index-linked are ones which rise automatically if inflation rises, and thus retain their purchasing power.

Indirect tax

An indirect tax is one that is not paid directly by a customer, but which is levied instead on the supplier, who passes it on to their customers in the form of higher prices. Insurance premium taxes, for example, are paid by the insurers, who then increase the premiums charged to their customers.

International Monetary Fund

The International Monetary Fund (IMF) is an international organisation that tries to stabilise the world economy and improve the economies of its members. The governments of most countries participate in it, with voting strength roughly proportional to their contributions to it. The IMF makes loans to those facing economic difficulties, subject to their following its recommendations.

Investment bank

Investment banks service companies, sometimes governments, and very wealthy private investors; they do not accept deposits and so are different to retail banks. Their other area of activity is trading securities. They take on larger risks than most retail banks, and can make bigger profits.

Investment fund

An investment fund manages the money from several investors, putting it into a variety of assets such as shares and bonds in order to achieve the balance of returns and security sought by its clients.

Junk bonds

Junk bonds are low quality bonds that carry a high risk of default and therefore offer high interest returns. They are rated as BB status or lower.

Leverage

(See 'Gearing')

LIBOR

LIBOR is the average interest rate at which banks lend to each other, and is declared by the British Bankers' Association on a daily basis. The initials stand for London Inter Bank Offered Rate.

Limited liability

Limited liability is the company status that limits a firm's liability and the claims made against it to the capital invested in the business. It protects the outside wealth of investors by confining their liability to the amount they put into the company.

Liquidity

Liquidity represents the ease with which something can readily be exchanged for cash. Property, for example, might take weeks or months to sell, so is relatively illiquid. Gold, by contrast, can be taken into a high street jewellers and exchanged for cash on the spot, and is therefore more liquid.

Macroeconomics

Macroeconomics deals with the broad economic aggregates such as employment levels, total annual investment, output and consumption. Macroeconomic policy attempts to steer the economy by altering the broad aggregates such as total government spending and money supply.

Manufactured goods

Manufactured goods are those which have physical form. They are usually contrasted with service industries which involve people doing things for one another without physical goods changing hands. A car is a manufactured good, whereas driving lessons are a service.

Market

A market is formed by the interaction of buyers and sellers. Their various transactions cumulatively establish current prices, although these change constantly as supply and demand change. People talk of 'the markets' to mean the sum of this activity, and take the prices at which people actually buy and sell to indicate the actions and sentiments of those engaged in market activity as opposed to the views of political leaders.

Market failure

Market failure is said to occur when various factors prevent the market from operating fairly or efficiently. There might be structural rigidities such as immobility of labour, or cartels maintaining prices above competitive levels. Governments often use market failure to justify intervention, although critics claim that government failure is no less common.

Microeconomics

Microeconomics looks at the economy in terms of the decisions made by individuals and businesses and the way in which they interact with one another to determine price levels and to create investment and job opportunities.

Monetary policy

Monetary policy is used when central banks and governments attempt to regulate inflation and currency exchange rates by controlling the money supply. This is often done by altering interest rates. Higher rates usually mean less money and credit to control inflation, plus a stronger currency, and damp down the economy. Lower rates do the reverse.

Money supply

The money supply is the total amount of money in a country's economy. This includes the cash circulated by its citizens, plus the money in their bank and savings accounts. It can be increased or decreased by governments and central banks. Too much money leads to inflation, and too little might stifle economic growth, so a careful balance has to be struck.

Monopoly

Monopoly happens where only one supplier is marketing a product or service, and thus faces no competitive pressures. Monopoly usually results in higher prices than those on a competitive market.

National debt

The national debt is the total debt owed by a government, and consists of all the IOUs it has issued in the form of bonds, notes, and other liabilities. Any annual budget deficit increases the national debt.

Negative equity

Negative equity describes the circumstance in which a home-buyer owes more on their home than the stake they own in it. Most home buyers have mortgages on their homes. As they repay some of their mortgage, their share of the home's worth (their equity in it) rises. If the home's value falls, however, they can be left owing more money than the home is now worth, and thus have negative equity.

Nominal value

The nominal value of an asset is the value it is declared to have, as opposed to its real value when bought and sold. Nominal value is sometimes called 'face' value or 'book' value, and is understood to be its value in name only. A bond issued at £100 has a nominal value of £100, though it might later change hands for much more or less than this.

Organisation for Economic Co-operation and Development

The Organisation for Economic Co-operation and Development (OECD) is an association of 34 countries including many from Europe together with the USA, Australia, New Zealand, Canada, Japan and Chile. Its purpose is to promote the economic development and well-being of its members by monitoring their performance, and to anticipate and prepare for future trends.

Portfolio

A portfolio is the collection of investments and assets that an individual owns. This might include shares, bonds and perhaps property.

Price/earnings ratio

The price/earnings (P/E) ratio gives investors information about a company's financial health and prospects. It is calculated by dividing the price of a company's shares by the earnings per share.

Quota

A quota is a limit put by government on the quantity of particular goods that may be imported into a country or trading bloc. It is sometimes used if the price of the imports is thought to be unfairly low because of subsidies, but its aim is always to protect domestic manufacturers or producers against cheaper foreign competition.

Rating

Rating is done by independent agencies such as Standard & Poor's and Moody's, who rate bonds according to their estimated risk of default. The ratings affect the interest rates which governments have to pay on the bonds they issue, with lower interest on the most secure ones.

Real terms

'In real terms' means after being adjusted to take inflation into account. If someone earns twice what they did a decade ago, but prices have doubled in the interim, then in real terms they are no better off. Economic statistics often present values in the currency level of a chosen year to eliminate the effects of inflation.

Recession

Recession occurs when an economy contracts instead of expanding, when it becomes less prosperous instead of more prosperous over time. The definition in most advanced countries is that two consecutive quarters (three-monthly periods) of lower economic output mean a country is officially in recession.

Retail Price Index

The Retail Price Index (RPI) is, like the Consumer Price Index (CPI), a measure of the changes over time in the price of a basket of typical goods. Unlike the CPI, it includes housing costs, and is therefore thought by some to be a more accurate measure of the actual cost of living.

Rights issue

A rights issue is used by a company to raise capital by issuing new shares. It gives current shareholders the right to buy a certain number of them at a fixed price on a specified date, and differs in this way from a share offering to the public at large.

Securities

Securities are the tradable documents that represent financial value. Typically they might be share certificates or bonds.

Selling short

Selling short, also called shorting, is done by traders who sell items they do not own, hoping that by the time they have to deliver they will be able to buy them at a lower price. Sometimes the action of selling short, especially if done by many people, might be enough to push the price of the item down.

Service industries

Service industries are those in which people perform services for each other without physical goods changing hands. Teachers and travel agents are both service occupations. A distinction is made between manufacturing and service industries because the former is more exposed to international competition from emerging economies than are service industries.

Small and Medium Enterprises (SMEs)

Small and Medium Enterprises, commonly known as SMEs, are businesses that fall below set limits in terms of either their total workforce or their annual turnover. In some countries they are given lighter tax or regulatory burdens because they are recognised as an important source of job creation.

Stagflation

Stagflation is the combination of economic stagnation with inflation. Governments used to think that inflation was a trade-off against unemployment, with more of one meaning less of the other. However, stagflation, in which there is both high inflation and high unemployment, shows this to be untrue.

Stock

Stock commonly refers to the original capital of a business. Ownership of part of a company's stock is denoted by share certificates, making 'stocks' and 'shares' virtually interchangeable in modern usage. A second meaning of 'stock' denotes the merchandise that a business has in hand, ready to sell. It has these goods 'in stock'.

Sub-prime mortgages

Sub-prime mortgages are home loans given to people who have lower incomes and are less likely to repay them. Some governments, anxious to extend home ownership, have encouraged sub-prime lending, offering guarantees to lenders to cover the greater risks of default.

Subsidy

A subsidy is the payment given by government to its domestic producers to enable them to stay in business against foreign competitors. It is often paid to industries in decline, or to farmers to achieve self-sufficiency in food production. Many subsidies are now contrary to WTO rules.

Tax avoidance

Tax avoidance is the expression for when taxpayers use legal loopholes such as trust funds, tax shelters or foreign location to keep down their tax liability. It is perfectly legal.

Tax evasion

The phrase tax evasion is used when people fail to declare economic activity such as earnings or capital gains in order to escape payment of the tax that is due. Evasion, unlike avoidance, is against the law.

Terms of trade

The terms of trade refer to the difference between what a country's imports cost on average, and the price its exports achieve. For some countries the terms of trade depend on how much they can sell their raw commodities for, versus what they have to pay for manufactured imports. When the balance is positive, the terms of trade are called favourable; when it is negative they are called adverse.

Treasury bill

A Treasury bill is a government IOU that matures within a year. They are sold at a price lower than the sum to be paid on maturity, with the difference representing the interest the government is paying on the loan.

Underwriters

Underwriters are the investment banks or syndicates of banks who underwrite new securities issues (e.g. shares or bonds), taking the risk of distributing them. Should investors fail to take up the shares at the offered price, the underwriters are pledged to do so.

Venture capital

Venture capital is the investment provided to new companies at an early stage of their development. The investors take an equity stake in return for supporting a company with development funds. These often feature high-risk companies bringing out unproven new technologies.

World Bank

The World Bank is the international bank owned by its member countries which exists to lend funds to less developed nations in order to assist their economic growth and development.

Word Trade Organization

The World Trade Organization (WTO) is the body that oversees the rules relating to international trade. Countries which join gain huge advantages of access to its markets, but have to abide by its strictures against unfair trading by such things as subsidies and tariffs.

INDEX

W

Z

MILTON FRIEDMAN

by Eamonn Butler

Milton Friedman changed the world. From free markets in China to the flat taxes of Eastern Europe, from the debate on drugs to monetary policy, Friedman's skill for vivid argument and ideas led to robust and often successful challenges to a dizzying amount of received wisdom.

In this brand new guide, find out:

- how Friedman undermined Keynesianism and the prevailing wisdom of large-scale economic intervention
- how he demonstrated the true cause of the Great Depression and identified its real culprits (they weren't the ones jumping out of the windows)
- what Friedman believed really destroys the value of the money in your pocket and how it can be stopped
- his arguments for why regulations and minimum-wage laws actually achieve lower standards and greater poverty
- his reasons for why big corporations prefer markets that aren't free, and how high taxation harms the wealthy less than anyone else.

With more, too, on democracy, equality, global trade, education, public services and financial crises, this is a concise but comprehensive guide to the influence of a key 20th century thinker.

www.harriman-house.com/miltonfriedman

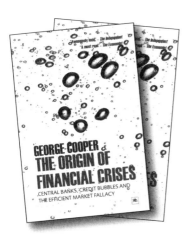

THE MYTH OF THE
RATIONAL
MARKET

by Justin Fox

"Valuable and highly readable"
– Wall Street Journal

"A must-read"
– New York Times

Chronicling the rise and fall of the efficient market theory and the century-long making of the modern financial industry, Justin Fox's *The Myth of the Rational Market* is as much an intellectual whodunit as a cultural history of the perils and possibilities of risk.

The book brings to life the people and ideas that forged modern finance and investing, from the formative days of Wall Street through the Great Depression and into the financial calamity of today.

It's a tale that features professors who made and lost fortunes, battled fiercely over ideas, beat the house in blackjack, wrote bestselling books, and played major roles on the world stage. It's also a tale of Wall Street's evolution, the power of the market to generate wealth and wreak havoc, and free market capitalism's war with itself.

www.harriman-house.com/
themythoftherationalmarket

Get the eBook version of *Economics Made Simple* for free

As a buyer of the printed version of *Economics Made Simple*, you can download the electronic version free of charge.

To get hold of your copy of the eBook, simply point your smartphone or tablet camera at the following (or go to **ebooks.harriman-house.com/ems**):

Hh Harriman House